THE CRUCIBLE

Arthur Miller

AUTHORED by Jeremy Ross
UPDATED AND REVISED by Elizabeth Weinbloom

COVER DESIGN by Table XI Partners LLC
COVER PHOTO by Olivia Verma and © 2005 GradeSaver, LLC

BOOK DESIGN by Table XI Partners LLC

Published by GradeSaver LLC, www.gradesaver.com

First published in the United States of America by GradeSaver LLC. 2000

GRADESAVER, the GradeSaver logo and the phrase "Getting you the grade
since 1999" are registered trademarks of GradeSaver, LLC

ISBN 978-1-60259-147-9

Printed in the United States of America

For other products and additional information please visit
http://www.gradesaver.com

Table of Contents

Table of Contents

Biography of Arthur Miller (1915-2005)

Arthur Miller was one of the leading American playwrights of the twentieth century. He was born in October 1915 in New York City to a women's clothing manufacturer, who lost everything in the economic collapse of the 1930s. Living through young adulthood during the Great Depression, then, Miller was shaped by the poverty that surrounded him. The Depression demonstrated to the playwright the fragility and vulnerability of human existence in the modern era. After graduating from high school, Miller worked in a warehouse so that he could earn enough money to attend the University of Michigan, where he began to write plays.

Miller's first play to make it to Broadway, The Man Who Had All the Luck (1944), was a dismal failure, closing after only four performances. This early setback almost discouraged Miller from writing completely, but, fortunately, he gave himself one more try. Three years later, All My Sons won the New York Drama Critics' Circle Award as the best play of 1947, launching Miller into theatrical stardom. All My Sons, a drama about a manufacturer of faulty war materials, was strongly influenced by the naturalist drama of Henrik Ibsen. Along with Death of a Salesman (his most enduring success), All My Sons and The Man Who Had All the Luck form a thematic trilogy of plays about love triangles involving fathers and sons. The drama of the family is at the core of all of Miller's major plays, but nowhere is it more prominent than in the realism of All My Sons and the impressionism of Death of a Salesman.

Death of a Salesman (1949) secured Miller's reputation as one of the nation's foremost playwrights. Death of a Salesman mixes the tradition of social realism that informs most of Miller's work with a more experimental structure that includes fluid leaps in time as the protagonist, Willy Loman, drifts into memories of his sons as teenagers. Loman represents an American archetype, a victim of his own delusions of grandeur and obsession with success, which haunt him with a sense of failure.

Miller won a Tony Award for Death of a Salesman as well as a Pulitzer Prize. The play has been frequently revived in film, television, and stage versions that have included actors such as Dustin Hoffman, George C. Scott and, most recently, Brian Dennehy in the part of Willy Loman.

Miller followed Death of a Salesman with his most politically significant work, The Crucible (1953), a tale of the Salem witch trials that contains obvious analogies to the McCarthy anti-Communist hearings in 1950s America. The highly controversial nature of the politics of The Crucible, which lauds those who refuse to name names, led to the play's mixed response. In later years, however, it has become one of the most studied and performed plays of American theater.

Three years after The Crucible, in 1956, Miller found himself persecuted by the very force that he warned against, when he was called to testify before the House

Un-American Activities Committee. Miller refused to name people he allegedly saw at a Communist writers' meeting a decade before, and he was convicted of contempt. He later won an appeal.

Also in 1956, Miller married actress Marilyn Monroe. The two divorced in 1961, the year of her death. That year Monroe appeared in her last film, The Misfits, which is based on an original screenplay by Miller. After divorcing Monroe, Miller wed Ingeborg Morath, to whom he remained married until his death in 2005. The pair had a son and a daughter.

Miller also wrote the plays A Memory of Two Mondays and the short A View from the Bridge, which were both staged in 1955. His other works include After the Fall (1964), a thinly veiled account of his marriage to Monroe, as well as The Price (1967), The Archbishop's Ceiling (1977), and The American Clock (1980). His most recent works include the plays The Ride Down Mt. Morgan (1991), The Last Yankee (1993), and Broken Glass (1993), which won the Olivier Award for Best Play.

Although Miller did not write frequently for film, he did pen an adaptation for the 1996 film version of The Crucible starring Daniel Day-Lewis and Winona Ryder, which garnered him an Academy Award nomination. Miller's daughter Rebecca married Day-Lewis in 1996.

About The Crucible

The Crucible is a fictional retelling of events in American history surrounding the Salem Witch Trials of the seventeenth century. Yet, is as much a product of the time in which Arthur Miller wrote it - the early 1950s - as it is description of Puritan society. The Salem witch trials took place from June through September of 1692, during which time nineteen men and women were hanged at Gallows Hill near Salem, while another man, Giles Corey, was stoned to death for refusing to submit to a trial on witchcraft charges. Hundreds of other persons faced accusations of witchcraft and dozens more languished in jail without trials. As the play describes, the witchcraft trials began because of the illness of Betty Parris, the daughter of the Salem minister, Reverend Samuel Parris, a former merchant in Barbados. Before Betty Parris fell ill, Cotton Mather had published "Memorable Providences," describing the suspected witchcraft of an Irish washerwoman in Boston, and Betty Parris' hysteria mirrored those of the suspected Irish witch. Other girls, including Ruth Putnam and Mercy Lewis also exhibited similar symptoms. However, actual events diverge from the narrative of the play. The Parris' slave, Tituba (who was likely a South American Arawak Indian and not African), immediately came under suspicion. As a form of counter-magic, Tituba was ordered to bake a rye cake with the urine of the afflicted victim and to feed the cake to a dog. This added to suspicions of witchcraft by Tituba, and led to the slave becoming one of the first women accused, along with Sarah Good and Sarah Osburn. Although most of the women first accused of witchcraft were considered disreputable, several reputable members of the community were soon executed, including Rebecca Nurse (featured in the play), and in the most controversial execution, George Burroughs, the former minister in Salem. One of the most flamboyant of the women executed was Bridget Bishop, a woman who had been married several times and was known as the mistress of two Salem taverns and had a reputation for dressing more 'artistically' than the women of the village.

Sir William Phips, the Governor of Massachusetts, created a new court to oversee the witchcraft cases. The Chief Justice of this court was William Stoughton, an avid witch-hunter who permitted many questionable deviations from normal courtroom procedure including the admission of spectral evidence (testimony by afflicted persons that they had been visited by a suspect's specter) and private conversations between accusers and judges.

By the early autumn of 1692, the cries of witchcraft began to ebb and doubts began to develop concerning the validity of the charges. Soon, the educated elite of the colony began efforts to end the witch-hunting hysteria that had enveloped Salem. Increase Mather, the father of Cotton, published "Cases of Conscience," which argued that it "were better that ten suspected witches should escape than one innocent person should be condemned." Mather urged the court to exclude spectral evidence. A period of atonement soon occurred in which Samuel Sewall, one of the judges, issued a public confession of guilt and apology, and Reverend Parris admitted errors in judgment. He did, however, attempt to shift the blame to others. (Governor Phips, for instance, shifted the blame to Stoughton, who nevertheless became the next Governor of Massachusetts.)

However, Miller wrote The Crucible not simply as a straight historical play detailing the Salem witch trials. Indeed, a good deal of the information in the play misrepresents the literal events of the trial: John Proctor was not a farmer, not a tavern owner, and during the time of the trials he was sixty years old and Abigail Williams only eleven. Rather, the play has as much significance as a product of the early Cold War era during which Miller wrote the play. Indeed, the play is a parable for the McCarthy era, in which similar 'witch hunts' occurred targeting citizens as communists rather than disciples of Satan.

Wisconsin Senator Joseph McCarthy was an undistinguished member of the Senate until February 1950, when he made the public charge that 205 Communists had infiltrated the State department. Upon subsequent testimony before the Senate Committee on Foreign Relations, McCarthy proved unable to produce the name of any "card-carrying" communists, but he gained increasing popular support for his campaign of accusations. Although he was later denounced, he promoted unfounded accusations and suspicions of communism in many quarters, and is best known for his investigation of communists in the United States Army.

The House Committee on Un-American Activities (generally known as HUAC) also investigated communism within Hollywood, calling a number of playwrights, directors and actors known for left-wing views to testify. Although some of these, including film director Elia Kazan, testified for the committee to avoid prison sentences, the Hollywood Ten, a group of entertainers, refused to testify and were convicted of contempt and sentenced to up to one year in prison. Over three hundred other entertainers were placed on a blacklist for possible communist views and were thus forbidden to work for major Hollywood studios (many of these were writers who worked under pseudonyms at the time, including Dalton Trumbo and Michael Wilson). Arthur Miller was one of these blacklisted. The blacklist prevented these men from receiving screen credit during this time, until actor Kirk Douglas pushed for Trumbo to receive screen credit for his adaptation of Spartacus for Stanley Kubrick in 1960.

About The Crucible

Character List

John Proctor

A farmer in Salem, Proctor serves as the voice of reason and justice in The Crucible. It is he who exposes the girls as frauds who are only pretending that there is witchcraft, and thus becomes the tragic hero of the tale. Proctor is a sharply intelligent man who can easily detect foolishness in others and expose it, but he questions his own moral sense. Because of his affair with Abigail Williams, Proctor questions whether or not he is a moral man, yet this past event is the only major flaw attributed to Proctor, who is in all other respects honorable and ethical. It is a sign of his morality that he does not feel himself adequate to place himself as a martyr for the cause of justice when he is given the choice to save himself at the end of the play.

Elizabeth Proctor

The wife of John Proctor, Elizabeth shares with John a similarly strict adherence to justice and moral principles She is a woman who has great confidence in her own morality and in the ability of a person to maintain a sense of righteousness, both internal and external, even when this principle conflicts with strict Christian doctrine. Although she is regarded as a woman of unimpeachable honesty, it is this reputation that causes her husband to be condemned when she lies about his affair with Abigail, thinking it will save him. However, Elizabeth can be a cold and demanding woman, whose chilly demeanor may have driven her husband to adultery and whose continual suspicions of her husband render their marriage tense.

Abigail Williams

A seventeen year-old girl who is the niece of Reverend Parris, Abigail was the Proctors' servant before Elizabeth fired her for having an affair with John. She is a malicious, vengeful girl who, in an attempt to protect herself from punishment after Reverend Parris finds them dancing, instigates the Salem witch trials and leads the charge of accusations. Despite her accusations, Abigail is an unabashed liar who charges witchcraft against those who oppose her, even Elizabeth Proctor in an attempt to take her place as Proctor's wife. Abigail's callous nature stems partially from past trauma; she is an orphan who watched as her parents were murdered by Indians.

Deputy Governor Danforth

The deputy governor of Massachusetts presides over the Salem witch trials. He is a stern yet practical man more interested in preserving the dignity and stature of the court than in executing justice or behaving with any sense of fairness. He approaches the witchcraft trials with a strict adherence to rules and law that obscure any sense of rationality, for under his legal dictates an accusation of witchery automatically entails a conviction. Danforth shows that his greatest interest is preserving the reputation of the court when he prompts Proctor to sign a confession, thus precluding the backlash of his execution.

Reverend Samuel Parris

A weak, paranoid and suspicious demagogue, Parris instigates the witchcraft panic when he finds his daughter and niece dancing in the woods with several other girls. Parris is continually beset with fears that others conspire against him. Parris knows the truth that Abigail is lying about the dancing and the witchcraft, but perpetuates the deception because it is in his own self interest. Parris fears any defense against the charges of witchcraft as an attack upon the court and a personal attack on him. As a pastor, his primary concern is personal aggrandizement - he strives for monetary compensation, including the deed to the preacher's house and expensive candlesticks.

Reverend John Hale

A scholar from Beverly, Reverend Hale comes to Salem on Reverend Parris' request to investigate supernatural causes for Betty Parris' suspicious illness and thus instigates the rumors of witchcraft. Hale approaches the situation precisely and intellectually, believing that he can define the supernatural in definitive terms. Despite his early enthusiasm for discerning the presence of witchcraft in Salem, Hale soon grows disillusioned with the witchcraft accusations that abound and defends Proctor when he challenges Abigail. Hale does this out of guilt, for he fears that he may have caused the execution of innocent persons.

Giles Corey

An irascible and combative old resident of Salem, Giles Corey is a comic figure in The Crucible whose fate turns tragic when he unwittingly effects his wife's charge for witchcraft when he wonders aloud about the strange books she reads at night. Corey is a frequent plaintiff in court, having brought dozens of lawsuits, and he stands with Proctor in challenging the girls' accusations, believing that Thomas Putnam is using charges of witchcraft to secure land. When Corey refuses to name the person who heard Putnam declare these intentions, Corey is charged with contempt of court and dies when the court orders him to be weighted with stones to coerce him to admit the name.

Mary Warren

The eighteen year-old servant in the Proctor household, Mary is one of the girls found dancing in the woods and is complicit in Abigail Williams' schemes. Although weak and tentative, she challenges the Proctors when they forbid her to go to court. However, Mary eventually breaks down and testifies against Abigail until Abigail charges her with witchery. She is a pliable girl whose actions are easily determined by others.

Tituba

Parris' slave from Barbados, Tituba was with the girls when they danced and attempted to conjure the spirits of Ann Putnam's dead children. She is the first person accused of witchcraft and likewise the first person to accuse others of witchery - particularly when she discovers that the easiest way to spare herself is to admit to the charges no matter their truth.

Thomas Putnam

One of the wealthiest landowners in Salem, Thomas Putnam is a vindictive, bitter man who holds longstanding grudges against many of the citizens of Salem, including the Nurse family for blocking the appointment of his brother-in-law to the position of minister. Putnam pushes his daughter to charge witchcraft against George Jacobs, for if he is executed, his land will be open for Putnam to purchase.

Rebecca Nurse

One of the most noble and well-respected citizens of Salem, this elderly woman is kindly and sane, suggesting that Betty's illness is simply a product of being out too late in the cold. However, because she served as midwife to Mrs. Putnam, Rebecca Nurse is charged with the supernatural murder of Putnam's children, who were each stillborn. Rebecca Nurse is the clear martyr in the play, the most pure and saintly character hanged for witchery.

Judge Hathorne

Hathorne is the judge who presides over the Salem witch trials. He remains largely subservient to Deputy Governor Danforth, but applies the same tortured reasoning to charges of witchcraft.

Francis Nurse

Francis is the husband of Rebecca Nurse, and a well-respected wealthy landowner in Salem. Francis Nurse joins Giles Corey and John Proctor in their challenge against the court when their respective wives are charged with witchcraft.

Betty Parris

The young teenager daughter of Reverend Parris, Betty falls mysteriously ill after Reverend Parris finds her dancing in the woods with Abigail and the other young women of Salem. She goes into hysterics when the charges of witchcraft first form, holding delusions that she can fly and exclaiming with horror when she hears the name of Jesus.

Sarah Good

One of the first women charged with witchery by the girls, she is a homeless woman who confesses to witchcraft to save herself and continues the charade with Tituba, comically claiming that Satan will take her and Tituba to Barbados.

Ezekiel Cheever

Ezekiel is a clerk of the court who serves the arrest warrants to the persons charged with witchcraft.

Mrs. Ann Putnam

The wife of Thomas Putnam, Ann suspects that there is some paranormal reason for the stillborn deaths of seven of her children and blames Rebecca Nurse.

Mercy Lewis

Mercy Lewis is the Putnam's servant - a fat, sly merciless eighteen year-old girl whom Parris found naked when he spied the girls dancing in the woods. She runs away with Abigail at the end of the play.

Susanna Walcott

Susanna is one of the girls whom Parris found dancing in the woods, and a confidant of Abigail.

Marshal Herrick

Marshal is one of the local constables who guards the jail cells while nearly drunk.

Hopkins

Hopkins is one of the guards at the jail cell.

Major Themes

Authority and Dissent

There are many levels of authority within the world of the Crucible. Early on, the Reverend Parris is the sole authoritative voice in Salem, as the minister and a graduate of Harvard College. He is supplanted by the arrival of Reverend Hale, who derives his authority from books and learning, which are then further supplanted in turn by the courts and its officials. Meanwhile, individualists like Proctor and Giles Corey rankle under these layers of authority – Proctor had long rejected Parris's preachings, and Corey made the authority of the law work for him as a constant plaintiff. But being an outlier is seen as dangerous in this society. Indeed, dissent against official authority is akin to being an anarchist at best and an agent of Satan at worst. Proctor and Corey are the two most modern figures in the play for their willingness to push back against the extreme authority of the courts. For this, however, they also suffer greatly.

Martyrdom

Miller addresses the question of whether a martyr must be a saint by having Proctor grapple with this very issue throughout the play. The early victims of the witch hunt are not seen as martyrs because even after death, they are considered undesired members of society. In contrast, the execution of Rebecca Nurse is widely recognized as one of martyrdom, because she has lived a conspicuously upright life and thus walks to the gallows without protest. Proctor sees himself as the borderline case – a respected member of society but far from sinless. It is only by recognizing that he need not be as perfect as Goody Nurse that Proctor finally finds "his goodness" as a moral man.

Community vs Individual

Salem is a tight-knit community where there is no such thing as private business. Individual activities like church attendance or book reading or keeping poppets become admissible evidence in court. Miller speculates that the community of Salem sought to keep itself together by casting out undesirable individuals, and in so doing created the atmosphere necessary for the witch hunts. The court itself was an extension of this principle, desperately in search of external validity – Danforth cannot possibly exonerate some when others have already perished for the same crime. But for the accused, it is only the individual that matters. In the end, Proctor is left with nothing but his name and reputation.

Naming Names

By requiring the accused to name others in their confessions, a witch hunt like that in Salem or HUAC can take on the form of a pyramid scheme or chain letter. In other words, to avoid the effects of this curse, you must pass it on to five other people, and so forth. This "naming names" allowed the accusations to spread and spread, while also permitting the public airing of grievances and sins. As a member of the blacklist himself, Miller felt particularly strongly about the evil of fingering others to save oneself, and he expresses this idea by having several characters grapple with the requirement that they name names. Giles Corey is held in contempt – the charge that ultimately leads to his execution – for refusing to name the person who told him of Putnam's scheming, and Proctor balks at the court's intention to question the 91 people who signed his declaration of the good character of the accused. But it is at the climax that this theme truly comes to the fore, as Proctor would rather die than accuse more innocent people.

Sin and Guilt

Miller identifies the witch hunt as an opportunity for the repressed members of Salem society to publicly proclaim both their own sins and the sins of others. Guilt has been bottled up at home in this community, and the airing of sins and grievances is a relief to those previously without an outlet for confession. Guilt motivates not only the witch hunts themselves, but also the behavior of several principal characters. Proctor is haunted by remorse over his infidelity, while Reverend Hale works to undermine the court that he helped create as penance for his sins. The ultimate irony of the Salem witch hunts is not only that the sins of the trials quickly outpaced the original crime, but that there was no original crime to begin with. Indeed, the abstract concept of sin was made concrete through compounding avoidances of guilt.

Self interest

In varying degrees, the instigators of the witch trials are working to serve their own self-interest. Abigail begins the hysteria when she finds it a convenient way to deflect attention from her own sins, and further points the accusations at Elizabeth to scheme her way into Proctor's arms. Tituba, the first charged, is also the first to confess when she realizes that a confession will save her life. Parris at first rankles against the witchcraft talk because it would undermine his reputation in the town, and later opposes the execution of prominent community members because their death would lead to popular uprising. Even Giles Corey died in the way he did because it was in his own interest – by not pleading and dying under the weighted rocks, he ensured that his property would pass to his sons rather than to the state.

Reputation

The reputation of each individual within the Salem community largely dictated his or her fate. The witch trials featured significant subversions of the dominant social structure by elevating to a position of power individuals whose reputation and status were otherwise lowly. Abigail, an unmarried, female orphan, suddenly became the most important person in town, bringing with her a dozen other such girls who otherwise could only hope to work as housekeepers until they married. Similarly, the black slave Tituba, whose race gave her the lowest social status in

Salem, found herself with the ability to decide the fates of people far more powerful than herself as she accused others of witchcraft. Conversely, individuals with sparkling reputations like Rebecca Nurse and Elizabeth Proctor were dragged through the mud and lost all agency in their situations. John Proctor is the appropriate protagonist for this story especially because he falls in the center of Salem's spectrum of reputation. As a landowner and adulterer, he is placed by Miller at the eye of the storm, watching the entire social structure pivot around him.

Glossary of Terms

adamant

utterly unyielding in attitude or opinion in spite of all appeals, urgings, etc

affidavit

a written declaration upon oath made before an authorized official

autocracy

government in which one person has uncontrolled or unlimited authority over others; the government or power of an absolute monarch

bowlegged

outward curvature of the legs causing a separation of the knees when the ankles are close or in contact

clod

A lump or chunk, especially of earth or clay

contention

a struggling together in opposition; strife

contiguous

touching; in contact.

Crucible

A container used for heating substances to high temperatures. Also a severe test or trial.

defamation

the act of defaming; false or unjustified injury of the good reputation of another, as by slander or libel; calumny

deposition

a statement under oath, taken down in writing, to be used in court in place of the spoken testimony of the witness

excommunicate

to cut off from communion with a church or exclude from the sacraments of a church by ecclesiastical sentence

faction

party strife and intrigue; dissension

gibbet

a gallows with a projecting arm at the top, from which the bodies of criminals were formerly hung in chains and left suspended after execution.

grapple

to seize another, or each other, in a firm grip, as in wrestling; clinch

intimation

to indicate or make known indirectly; hint; imply; suggest.

lechery

unrestrained or excessive indulgence of sexual desire

licentious

sexually unrestrained; lascivious; libertine; lewd.

magistrate

A civil officer charged with administration of the law

obscene

offensive to morality or decency; indecent; depraved

pallor

unusual or extreme paleness, as from fear, ill health, or death; wanness

parish

a local church with its field of activity

pilgrimage

any long journey, esp. one undertaken as a quest or for a votive purpose, as to pay homage

plaintiff

a person who brings suit in a court

poppet

a doll

predilection

A preference, or partiality

pretense

pretending or feigning; make-believe

prodigious

extraordinary in size, amount, extent, degree, force, etc

propriety

conformity to established standards of good or proper behavior or manners.

providence

a manifestation of divine care or direction

reproach

to find fault with (a person, group, etc.); blame; censure.

struck dumb

rendered mute, unable to speak

subservient

serving or acting in a subordinate capacity; subordinate

titillated

aroused

trepidation

tremulous fear, alarm, or agitation; perturbation

vengeance

infliction of injury, harm, humiliation, or the like, on a person by another who has been harmed by that person; violent revenge

Short Summary

The Crucible, a historical play based on events of the Salem witchcraft trials, takes place in a small Puritan village in the colony of Massachusetts in 1692. The witchcraft trials, as Miller explains in a prose prologue to the play, grew out of the particular moral system of the Puritans, which promoted interference in others' affairs as well as a repressive code of conduct that frowned on any diversion from norms of behavior.

The play begins in the home of Reverend Samuel Parris, whose daughter, Betty, lays ill. Parris lives with his daughter and his seventeen-year old niece, Abigail Williams, an orphan who witnessed her parents' murder by the Indians. Parris has sent for Reverend Hale of Beverly, believing his daughter's illness stems from supernatural explanations. Betty became ill when her father discovered her dancing in the woods with Abigail, Tituba (the Parris' slave from Barbados) and several other local girls. Already there are rumors that Betty's illness is due to witchcraft, but Parris tells Abigail that he cannot admit that he found his daughter and niece dancing like heathens in the forest. Abigail says that she will admit to dancing and accept the punishment, but will not admit to witchcraft. Abigail and Parris discuss rumors about the girls: when they were dancing one of the girls was naked, and Tituba was screeching gibberish. Parris also brings up rumors that Abigail's former employer, Elizabeth Proctor, believes that Abby is immoral.

Thomas and Ann Putnam arrive and tell Parris that their daughter, Ruth, is sick. Ann Putnam admits that she sent Ruth to Tituba, for Tituba knows how to speak to the dead and could find out who murdered her seven children, each of whom died during infancy. When the adults leave, Abigail discusses Betty's illness with Mercy Lewis and Mary Warren, the servants of the Putnams and the Proctors, respectively. Abigail threatens them, warning them not to say anything more than that they danced and Tituba conjured Ruth's sisters. John Proctor arrives to find Mary and send her home. He speaks with Abigail alone, and she admits to him about the dancing. In the past, John and Abigail had an affair, which is the reason why Elizabeth Proctor fired her. Abigail propositions John, but he sternly refuses her. When Betty hears people singing psalms from outside, she begins to shriek. Reverend Parris returns, and realizes that Betty cannot bear to hear the Lord's name.

Giles Corey and Rebecca Nurse are the next to visit. The former is a contentious old man, while the latter is a well-respected old woman. Rebecca claims that Betty's illness is nothing serious, but merely a childish phase. Parris confronts Proctor because he has not been in church recently, but Proctor claims that Parris is too obsessed with damnation and never mentions God.

Reverend John Hale arrives from Beverly, a scholarly man who looks for precise signs of the supernatural. Parris tells him about the dancing and the conjuring, while Giles Corey asks if there is any significance to his wife's reading strange books. Hale questions Abigail, asking if she sold her soul to Lucifer. Finally Abigail blames Tituba, claiming that Tituba made Abigail and Betty drink blood and that Tituba sends her spirit out to make mischief. Putnam declares that Tituba must be hanged, but Hale confronts her. Upon realizing that the only way to save herself is to admit to the charge, Tituba claims that the devil came to her and promised to return her to Barbados. She says that several women were with him, including Sarah Good and Sarah Osburn, and the girls join in the chorus of accusations, name more people they claim to have seen with the devil.

The second act takes place a week later in the Proctor's home. John Proctor returns home late after a long day planting in the fields, and Elizabeth suspects that he has been in the village. Mary Warren has been there as an official of the court for the witchcraft trials, even after Elizabeth forbade her. Elizabeth tells John that she must tell Ezekiel Cheever, the constable, that Abigail admitted that Betty's sickness has nothing to do with witchcraft, but Proctor admits that nobody will believe him because he was alone with Abigail at the time. Elizabeth is disturbed by this, but Proctor reprimands her for her suspicion. Mary Warren arrives and gives Elizabeth a poppet that she made in court. Mary tells them that thirty-nine people have been arrested and Sarah Osburn will hang, but not Sarah Good, who confessed. When Proctor becomes angry at Mary, she tells him that she saved Elizabeth's life today, for her name was mentioned in court.

John Hale arrives. He tells the Proctors that Rebecca Nurse was charged, then questions Proctor on his churchgoing habits. Finally he makes Proctor state the ten commandments; he can remember nine of the ten, but Elizabeth must remind him of adultery. Proctor tells Hale what Abigail admitted about Parris discovering her in the woods, but Hale says that it must be nonsense, for so many have confessed to witchcraft. Proctor reminds him that these people would certainly confess, if denying it means that they be hanged. Hale asks Proctor whether he believes in witches, and he says that he does, but not those in Salem. Elizabeth denies all belief in witchcraft, for she believes that the devil cannot take a woman's soul if she is truly upright.

Ezekiel Cheever arrives to arrest Elizabeth on the charge that she sent her spirit out to Abigail and stuck a needle in her. Cheever finds the poppet, which has a needle in it, but Mary Warren says that she made the poppet in court that day, although Abigail witnessed her making it. Upon hearing the charge, Elizabeth claims that Abigail is a murderer who must be ripped out of the world. Proctor rips up the warrant and tells Cheever that he will not give his wife to vengeance. When Hale insists that the court is just, Proctor calls him a Pontius Pilate. He finally demands that Mary Warren come to court and testify against Abigail, but she sobs that she cannot.

The third act takes place in the vestry room of the Salem meeting house, which serves the court. Giles Corey arrives with Francis Nurse and tells Deputy Governor Danforth, who presides over the trials, that Thomas Putnam is charging people with witchcraft in order to gain their land. He also says that he meant nothing when he said that his wife read strange books.

John Proctor arrives with Mary Warren, and presents a deposition signed by Mary that asserts that she never saw any spirits. Parris thinks that they are there to overthrow the court, and Danforth questions whether Proctor has any ulterior motive, and tells Proctor that his wife is pregnant and thus will live at least one more year, even if convicted. Proctor also presents a petition signed by ninety-one people attesting to the good character of Elizabeth Proctor, Rebecca Nurse and Martha Corey. Parris claims that this is an attack upon the court, but Hale asks Parris if every defense is an attack on it.

Putnam arrives at the court, and Giles Corey charges him with murder. Giles tells Danforth that someone told him that Putnam prompted his daughter to accuse George Jacobs so that he could buy his land. Giles refuses to name this person, and so is arrested for contempt. Abigail then arrives with the other girls, and Proctor tells Danforth how Abigail means to murder his wife. Abigail pretends that she feels a sharp wind threatening her. Proctor grabs her by the hair and calls her a whore, finally admitting his affair.

Danforth orders that Elizabeth be brought to the court. If Elizabeth admits to firing Abigail for her affair, Danforth will charge Abigail with murder. Elizabeth, thinking that she is defending her husband, only claims that she fired Abigail because of poor work habits. Proctor cries out for Elizabeth to tell the truth, and Hale admits that Elizabeth's lie is a natural one to tell. Abigail then claims that Mary Warren's spirit is attacking her in the form of a bird. Although Mary claims that the girls are lying, she soon breaks down and tells Danforth that Proctor is in league with Satan and wants to pull down the court. Proctor cries out that God is dead, and that a fire is burning in Hell because the court is pulling Heaven down and raising up a whore. Hale denounces the proceedings and quits the court.

The fourth act takes places several months later in the autumn at the Salem jail cell. Cheever details how the town is in shambles because so many people are in jail. Hale has been begging Rebecca Nurse to admit to witchcraft. Parris arrives and tells Danforth how Abigail has vanished with Mercy Lewis and stolen his money. Parris worries about the rumors of rebellion against the witchcraft proceedings in Andover, but Hathorne reminds Parris how there has only been great satisfaction in all of the Salem executions. Parris reminds him that Rebecca Nurse is no immoral woman like the others executed and there will be consequences to her execution. Still, Danforth refuses to postpone any of the executions.

Danforth calls for Elizabeth Proctor, and Hale tells her that he does not want Proctor to die, for he would feel responsible for the murder. He tells Elizabeth that God may damn a liar less than a person who throws one's life away, but Elizabeth claims that this may be the Devil's argument. Finally Elizabeth agrees to speak with Proctor, who is brought in bearded and filthy. Proctor and Elizabeth discuss their children, and Elizabeth tells him how Giles Corey died: when he refused to answer yes or no to his indictment, and was thus pressed with stones until he would answer. He only gave the words "more weight" before they crushed him.

Proctor says that he cannot mount the gibbet as a saint, for it would be a fraud to claim that he has never lied. Elizabeth says that she has her own sins, for only a cold wife would prompt lechery. Finally Proctor decides that he will confess himself. Danforth demands a written confession and, to prove the purity of his soul, he demands that Proctor accuse others. Hale suggests that it is sufficient for Proctor to confess to God, but Danforth still requires a written statement. Proctor refuses, because he wishes only to keep his good name for the respectability of his children. Danforth refuses to accept his confession, and orders that he be hanged. Hale begs Elizabeth to plead with Proctor to sign a confession, but Elizabeth claims that Proctor now has his goodness, and nobody should take it away from him.

Summary and Analysis of Act One

The play is set in Salem, Massachusetts in the spring of 1692, and the first act begins in a small upper bedroom of the home of Reverend Samuel Parris, who kneels in prayer at the bed of his daughter, Betty.

Tituba, Rev. Parris' slave from Barbados, enters the room. She is concerned for Betty's welfare, but Parris makes her leave. Abigail Williams, the niece of Rev. Parris, also enters, along with Susanna Walcott, who tells Rev. Parris that Dr. Griggs can find no cure for Betty's ailment. Parris has sent for Reverend Hale of Beverly, who will confirm the possibility of an unnatural cause of Betty's illness, but he orders Susanna to say nothing of unnatural causes to others. Abigail warns Parris that there are rumors of witchcraft and that the parlor is packed with people. Parris tells her that he cannot reveal that he found his daughter and niece dancing in the forest like heathens. Abigail admits to dancing and is willing to accept the punishment, but will not admit to witchcraft. Parris warns Abigail that he has enemies who will use this situation against him, and claims that he saw a dress lying on the grass and someone naked running through the trees. He thinks that Tituba was screeching gibberish when he found the girls, but Abigail says they were only singing Barbados songs. Parris demands to know whether Abigail has a good reputation, following up on rumors that her former employee, Goody Proctor, thinks Abigail is corrupt, but Abigail calls Goody Proctor a gossiping liar.

Mrs. Ann Putnam and Mr. Thomas Putnam enter; she claims that Betty's illness is certainly a stroke of hell. There are rumors that Betty was flying over the Ingersoll's barn, according to Mrs. Putnam. Their daughter Ruth is also sick, and they assume witchcraft to be the cause. Mrs. Putnam admits that she sent Ruth to Tituba. She believes that Tituba knows how to speak to the dead, and she wished to learn who murdered her seven children during their infancy.

The Putnams' servant, Mercy Lewis, arrives and visits Betty. She discusses Ruth's sickness with Abigail, and suggests beating Betty to snap her out of her illness. Abigail tells Ruth that Rev. Parris knows that Tituba conjured Ruth's sisters, and that Parris saw Mercy naked. Mary Warren, the Proctors' current servant, enters in a panic because the town is talking witchcraft. Betty suddenly sits up and cries that Abigail drank blood to kill Goody Proctor. Abigail threatens the other girls: if they say anything other than that they danced and Tituba conjured Ruth Putnam's sisters, Abigail will make their lives difficult.

John Proctor arrives and orders Mary Warren to go home. Abigail speaks tenderly to him and references an affair between them, but Proctor states that he will cut off his hand before he ever touches her again. As they hear the people downstairs sing a hymn downstairs, Abigail insists that Proctor loves her yet. He fends her off, firmly but not without sympathy. Hearing the hymn outside, Betty sits up and screams. Abigail calls for Rev. Parris, who believes that Betty cannot bear to hear the Lord's name.

The elderly Giles Corey enters with Rebecca Nurse, wife of Francis Nurse. Rebecca, who has eleven children and twenty-six grandchildren, claims that Betty's illness is nothing serious. She is skeptical of the claims of witchcraft. Putnam suspects Proctor, because he has not been at Sabbath recently, but Proctor claims there is no need for attendance since all Parris ever talks about are finances. Parris warns that there must be obedience or the church will burn like Hell, and Proctor wonders whether Parris can speak one minute without mentioning Hell.

Reverend John Hale of Beverly then arrives, bringing with him half a dozen heavy books. He introduces himself to Rebecca Nurse, and has heard of her great charity. Giles Corey tells Hale that Proctor does not believe in witches, but Proctor says he did not speak one way or another. Hale says that they cannot look to superstition in issues of witchcraft, because the Devil is precise. Parris admits to the dancing and the conjuring, while Mrs. Putnam claims that witchcraft must be the cause of death for her seven children. Giles Corey asks Hale what the reading of strange books signifies. He says that he often awakes to find Martha reading in a corner and cannot say his prayers, but Hale dismisses his concerns for the moment.

Hale asks Abigail what happened in the forest. Parris claims he saw a kettle, but Abigail says it contained only soup, although a frog may have jumped in it. Parris asks whether they drank anything in it, and Hale asks Abigail if she has sold her soul to Lucifer. Finally Abigail blames Tituba, claiming that Tituba made her and Betty drink chicken blood. Abigail says that Tituba sends her spirit on her in church and makes her laugh at prayer. Putnam declares that Tituba must be hanged. Hale confronts Tituba. He says that if she loves these children she must let God's light shine on her. Hale asks if the Devil comes to her with anybody else. Tituba admits that the devil has come to her, and that the devil promises to return her to Barbados. Furthermore, she shows how he has white people working for her, including Goody Good and Goody Osburn. Betty claims that she saw George Jacobs with the Devil, while Abigail claims she saw several others with the devil, and the curtain falls on a rising chorus of accusations.

Analysis

First performed in January of 1953 at the height of America's red scare, The Crucible is first and foremost a political argument, relating the Salem witchcraft trials to their contemporary equivalent in Miller's time. the McCarthy hearings. The figurative 'witch hunt' of McCarthyism becomes literal in Miller's play, which is constructed to illustrate how fear and hysteria mixed with an atmosphere of persecution may lead to tragically unjust consequences. Miller presents the play with traditional theatrical devices, relying on the dialogue and situations to illustrate his themes, but finds these somewhat insufficient. In the first act, the play therefore contains a number of historical digressions that reveal the motivations of each character and which cannot be accurately conveyed through a strict stage interpretation.

Through these prose passages that interrupt the dialogue and action of the play, Miller establishes the particular quality of Salem society that makes it particularly receptive to the repression and panic of the witch trials. The Puritan life in Salem is rigid and somber, allowing little room for people to break from the monotony and strict work ethic that dominated the close-knit society. Furthermore, the Puritan religious ethic informed all aspects of society, promoting safeguards against immorality at any cost to personal privacy or justice. The Puritans of Massachusetts were a religious faction who, after years of suffering persecution themselves, developed a willful sense of community to guard against infiltration from outside sources. It is this paradox that Miller finds to be a major theme of The Crucible: in order to keep the community together, members of that community believed that they must in some sense tear it apart. Miller relates the intense paranoia over the integrity of the Puritan community to their belief that they are in some sense a chosen people, who will forge a new destiny for the world. This relates strongly to the political climate of the early 1950s in which Miller wrote The Crucible. After the end of World War II, the United States found itself engaged in a struggle for political supremacy with Communist forces, in particular the Soviet Union. Just as the Salem authorities believed that witchcraft threatened their community, many Americans during this time saw Communism as a threat to the American way of life.

However, the Salem witch trials as described by Miller have a sexual element that runs concurrent with the political aspects of the allegory. The community is one that promotes interference in all personal matters and intensely frowns upon any sinful conduct, without allowing for any legitimate expurgation of sin. The witch trials serve as a means to break from this stifling atmosphere and publicly confess one's sins through accusation. This simultaneous fear of and fascination with sexuality is a theme throughout The Crucible, as demonstrated by the adulterous relationship between Abigail Williams and John Proctor and the sexual undertones of the dancing that instigates the witchcraft trials. The 1950s were likewise an era of sexual conservatism, and known or suspected homosexuals were at particular risk for being singled out as Communist sympathizers.

The first act establishes the primary characters of the play who instigate the Salem witch trials. Each has his particular obsessions and motivations that drive him to push for the trials. The first and perhaps most reprehensible of these characters is the Reverend Samuel Parris, a man who symbolizes the particular quality of moral repression and paranoia that drive the trials. Miller immediately establishes Parris as a man whose main concern is his reputation and status in the community, rather than the well-being of his daughter. It is Tituba who shows more concern for Betty than her father, but she is kept away from the girl's sick bed. When he discusses finding Abigail and Betty dancing in the woods, his concern is not the sin that they committed but rather the possibility that his enemies will use this scandal against him. Parris is distinctly paranoid, defending himself from all enemies even when they may not exist. The particular quality of Parris that renders him dangerous is his strong belief in the presence of evil. Even before the witchcraft paranoia, Proctor indicates that Parris showed an obsession with damnation and hell in order to strike fear into his parishioners. With the seeming presence of witchcraft in Salem, Parris now has a concrete, physical manifestation of the evil he so fears.

Abigail Williams is a less complex character whose motivations are simple; she is a clear villain with straightforward malicious motivation. Miller establishes that Abigail is suspected of adultery with John Proctor, a rumor that is confirmed later in the first act. Abigail demonstrates a great ability for self-preservation: she admits what she must at appropriate times, and places the blame for her actions at the most convenient source, Tituba. She then takes advantage of the situation to accuse Elizabeth Proctor, aiming to take her place in John Proctor's life. Abigail's lack of any morality renders her able to charge others with witchery no matter the consequences.

The third character who serves as a proponent of the witchcraft hysteria is Thomas Putnam. While Parris's motivation is suspicion and paranoia and Abigail's is mere villainy, Thomas Putnam demonstrates that his motivation involves his longstanding grudges against others; the witchcraft trials give Putnam an opportunity to exact revenge against others, and, as will later be shown, to profit economically from others' executions.

The final character who sets the witchcraft trials in motion is Reverend John Hale. Hale is perhaps the most complex character in The Crucible, a man who approaches religious matters with the conviction of a scientist and a scientific emphasis on proper procedure. Hale holds the contradictory belief that they cannot rely on superstition to solve the girls' problems but that they may find a supernatural explanation for the events. Since he lacks the malicious motivations and obsessions that plague the other instigators of the trials, Reverend Hale has the ability to change his position, yet at this point he finds himself caught up in the hysteria he has helped to create.

In contrast to these four characters stand the three main opponents of the witchcraft accusations. The Nurses are the most straightforward of these; Miller portrays Rebecca Nurse and her husband as near saints who rely on practical wisdom and experience. In contrast, Giles Corey has none of the noble character of the Nurses, yet he can oppose Parris and Putnam because of his contentious, combative manner. Giles Corey doesn't care about public opinion and has never allowed his actions to be swayed by those around him. He may therefore choose whichever position he finds most suitable, even if it places him in danger.

However, Miller places John Proctor as the main protagonist of the story and its moral center. Proctor, as Miller writes, is a man who can easily discern foolishness and has the will to oppose it. He is a rational man with a brusque manner who, like Giles Corey, has no qualms about expressing his opinion. Miller portrays Proctor as a decidedly modern character, who eschews superstition for rationality and expresses skepticism for the trappings of organized religion, particularly Parris's obsession with hellfire and damnation. The particularly modern quality of John Proctor draws the audience sympathy to him, even if he is a self-professed sinner who had an affair with Abigail Williams. Yet this is the single sin that Proctor manifests and exists more as a plot point than as an organic character trait. The Proctor that Miller portrays throughout The Crucible has succumbed to and overcome temptation, like so many of us, making him both flawed and respectable.

Several significant themes emerge early in the play. One of these that Miller develops throughout the first act is the speed at which gossip can spread in a close-knit society like Salem. Miller establishes Salem as a world in which little information is considered private; all information is open to suspicion and question. This correlates to the McCarthy hearings, which probed into the lives of the suspected communists for evidence of their anti-American activity, no matter the actual relevance.

A second theme that Miller establishes is the ability of people to choose whichever position suits their self-interest. Abigail Williams shows the ability to affirm or deny any charge against her based entirely on whether it serves her needs, while Tituba, when charged with witchcraft, denies it only until she realizes that admitting to the crime will save her from further punishment and that accusing others will shift the blame elsewhere. The shift of blame from one character to another will be a recurring plot point, as few characters will accept the consequences of their actions or directly confront the charges leveled against them.

Perhaps the most important theme that Miller develops in this act is the propensity of accusations to snowball. The charges against the girls and Tituba become perpetually more significant: at first they are accused of merely dancing, then of dancing naked. The charges proceed until Tituba is deemed a witch and accuses others of conspiring with Satan. Legitimate charges of dancing and sinful activity increase in magnitude until charges of Satanism arise. The irony of this situation is that the fight against sinfulness in Salem will become more sinful and malicious than any of the actual events that occurred – much like, in Miller's opinion, the McCarthy era did more to tear apart America than Communist sympathizers ever did.

Summary and Analysis of Act Two

The second act takes place in the common room of Proctor's house eight days later. John Proctor returns from a day in the fields and greets his wife, Elizabeth. They make small talk about dinner and the crops, but there is an awkwardness between them. Elizabeth thinks that he went to Salem that afternoon, but Proctor says he thought better of it. Elizabeth tells him that Mary Warren is there today, and although Elizabeth tried to forbid her, Mary frightened her strength away. Mary is now an official in the court, formally accusing people of witchcraft, along with Abigail and the other girls. Elizabeth tells John to go to Ezekiel Cheever and tell him what Abigail said last week - namely that Betty's sickness had nothing to do with witchcraft. Proctor tells her that nobody will believe him, as Proctor was the only one to hear.

Elizabeth is disturbed to realize that Proctor and Abigail were alone together, but Proctor angers at her suspicion. He has tiptoed around the house for the seven months since Abigail left, and has confessed to his sin openly, but Elizabeth remains cold. She claims she does not judge him. Proctor replies that her justice would freeze beer.

Mary Warren enters, and gives Elizabeth a poppet that she made in court that day. Mary reports that thirty-nine people are arrested, and Goody Osburn will hang, but not Sarah Good because she confessed. Mary Warren claims that Goody Osburn sent her spirit out in court to choke them, and often mumbles whenever others turn her away when she begs. Proctor demands proof that Goody Osburn is a witch, and forbids Mary Warren to go to court. Mary says that it is amazing that Proctor does not realize the importance of her work, and insists that she is a court official. Incensed, Proctor threatens her with a whip.

Mary reveals that she saved Elizabeth's life today, for Elizabeth was accused in court. Proctor orders Mary to go to bed. Elizabeth realizes that Abigail wants her dead. Proctor reassures her that he will find Ezekiel Cheever and tell him what Abigail said, but Elizabeth thinks that more than Cheever's help is needed now. She tells him to go to Abigail and firmly renege on whatever promise she may think he made her. Elizabeth believes Abigail must plan to profit from Elizabeth's death, for accusing a respected member of society like her is more dangerous than accusing a drunk or indigent woman like Good or Osburn.

Mr. Hale arrives at the house as Elizabeth and John argue over Abigail. He now has a quality of deference and even guilt. Hale tells them that Elizabeth's name was mentioned in court and Rebecca Nurse was charged. Proctor finds it impossible to believe that so pious a woman could be in the service of the devil after seventy years of prayer, but Hale reminds him that the Devil is wily and strong. Hale questions Proctor on his churchgoing habits, and Proctor claims that he prays at home and criticizes Parris for his wasteful spending habits in church. Hale also notes that only two of Proctor's children are baptized, and asks Proctor to state the Ten Commandments. He names nine of them, but needs Elizabeth to remind him of the tenth – adultery. Proctor says that between the two of them they know all of the Commandments, but Hale says that no crack in the fortress of theology can be considered small.

Proctor says there is no witchcraft happening, and tells Hale how Abigail said Parris discovered the girls sporting in the woods. Hale claims that it is nonsense, as so many have confessed, but Proctor says that anyone would confess if they will be hanged for denying it. Hale asks if Proctor will testify to this in court, and asks if he believes in witches. Proctor answers that he does not believe that there are witches in Salem, but Elizabeth denies any belief in witches at all. When Hale asks Elizabeth if she questions the gospel, she retorts that he should question Abigail Williams about the gospel and not her.

Giles Corey arrives with Francis Nurse, and they tell the Proctors that their wives were taken away. Rebecca has been charged with the supernatural murder of Ann Putnam's babies. Hale, who is deeply troubled, claims that if Rebecca Nurse is tainted, there is nothing to stop the whole world from burning. Walcott charged Martha Corey for the rumor that Giles proposed about his wife reading books.

Cheever arrives to charge Elizabeth. He asks if she keeps any poppets in the house, and she says no. Cheever spies the poppet that Mary Warren made, and finds a needle in it. Abigail had testified that Elizabeth's familiar spirit pushed a needle into her at dinner that night. Mary Warren tells them how the poppet got into the house, and claims that she stuck the needle in it, but Hale questions whether or not her memory is accurate or supernatural. Elizabeth, upon hearing that Abigail has charged her with murder, calls Abigail a murderer who must be ripped out of the world. Proctor rips up the warrant, and asks if the accuser is always holy now. He says that he will not give his wife to vengeance. Hale insists that the court is just, but Proctor calls him a Pontius Pilate. Cheever takes Elizabeth away. Proctor demands that Mary Warren come to court with him and charge murder against Abigail. She warns Proctor that Abigail will charge him with lechery, but Proctor insists that his wife shall not die for him. Mary Warren sobs that she cannot go against Abigail.

Analysis

While the first act takes place in the "public" setting of Reverend Parris' home, the second act moves into what should be considered the private sphere of the Proctors' home. The conversation between John and Elizabeth Proctor is highly mundane, illustrating the significant tension remaining in the relationship since Proctor's affair with Abigail Williams. Elizabeth Proctor is intensely suspicious of her husband, worrying when he arrives at home late for dinner and adopting a condescending tone when her husband admits that he was momentarily alone with Abigail Williams. Miller establishes Elizabeth Proctor as a morally upright woman, respectable and dignified, yet with an air of superiority that renders her frigid and distant. Proctor feels that Elizabeth has made her home into a repressive atmosphere, continually punishing her husband for his wrongdoing. Still, if Elizabeth adopts a tone of moral superiority it is because she is the superior of her contemporaries, with an unwavering belief in the capability of persons to remain moral.

Miller creates an atmosphere of guilt within the Proctor household that mirrors the similar conditions within larger Puritan society. Proctor has expressed contrition for his infidelity and asked for forgiveness, yet there is no sense of catharsis within his marriage nor ability for full reconciliation. The Proctor marriage is stagnant and stifling, as the fact of John's adultery lingers in every conversation like a giant white elephant. Miller demonstrates this, in particular, when Proctor is unable to recall the commandment against adultery – it is a moment of humor, but it also reflects the crisis of the Proctor marriage. Miller seems to indicate that, like the rest of their Puritan society, the Proctors need an outlet to expiate John's sins and without this means for redemption they are committed to a perpetual obsession with past infidelity.

Two major themes emerge in the second act of The Crucible. The first of these is the line between public and private. The act itself moves from the intimate conversation between husband and wife to more public matters, but the division between these two spheres becomes obscure. Even in this setting, the public discussions of the Proctors' guilt or innocence occurs within the home. More importantly, Reverend Hale and the other court officials use private information for their public matters, such as information about the frequency with which they attend church and their belief in the existence of witches. The court officials investigate all aspects of the suspects' private lives. Under such intense scrutiny, these officials are able to find any information that may be may interpreted as evidence of guilt – not unlike the House Unamerican Activities Commission using everything from religion and sexuality to, in the case of the Rosenbergs, a discarded box of Jell-o as evidence of un-American behavior.

The second major theme of the act is the ambiguity of evidence. This begins even before Hale arrives at the Proctors' home, when Elizabeth, as a betrayed wife, suspects her husband's excuses for coming home late. This continues with Reverend Hale's interpretation of John's forgetfulness of one of the Ten Commandments and the evidence against Martha Corey, which deemed her a witch for reading books. The most significant symbol of this theme in the second act is Mary Warren's poppet. Miller makes it clear to the audience that Elizabeth did not use the poppet as a charm against Abigail Williams, but its presence in her house is quite damning in the view of the court.

The poppet demonstrates that Abigail Williams is more villainous than earlier indicated. In the first act she behaved solely out of self-interest. She was ready to do harm to others, but only to save herself. However, in this instance she purposely frames Elizabeth Proctor out of revenge, planting the poppet as a means to engineer Elizabeth's murder. This event even breaks the icy exterior of Elizabeth Proctor, who deems that Abigail must be "ripped out of the world."

Miller creates a situation of bleak irony in this chapter with the arrest of Rebecca Nurse and Elizabeth Proctor. These characters are the most upright in the play, yet are accused of witchcraft by two of the most ignoble, Thomas Putnam and Abigail Williams. The dynamic of the witchcraft hysteria has created a situation in which the accuser of witchcraft is automatically presumed holy, as Proctor notes, while even the most spiritual character may be suspected of Satanic influence. In this situation the evil of Salem may raise their reputations at the expense of the good.

An additional irony that Miller constructs in the act is in the plot structure. The Proctors and their allies can rely on a single person to save themselves from Abigail Williams' treachery. Yet this person, Mary Warren, is the weakest and most pliable character in The Crucible. She alone has the power to stop the hysteria of the witchcraft trials, but neither the strength nor resolve to do so. Mary requires intense coercion from John Proctor to even consider admitting to the falsehood in court. However, despite her weakness Mary Warren is as dangerous as Abigail, for the guileless girl betrays none of Abigail's malicious bearing and thus appears more overtly innocent. She is a pawn who may be used by the Proctors to prove their innocence, but Miller foreshadows that Mary Warren may be used by Abigail to serve her own purposes as well.

Among the characters in the play, it is Reverend Hale who demonstrates the most prominent character development. While the other characters remain fixed in their particular allegiances and beliefs, Hale demonstrates the debilitating effects of the witchcraft trials by the change in his character. When he reappears in the third act he has none of his old enthusiasm. Although he clings to his belief that proof of witchery can be found in Salem, Hale appears more and more tentative about the results. He demonstrates a strong feeling of guilt for his actions, as shown by his reliance on what he grasps as indisputable evidence. Like Pontius Pilate, to whom Proctor compares Hale, he wants to play only a passive role in the proceedings without any feeling of personal responsibility. Hale's growing disillusionment foreshadows his later repudiation of the court's actions.

Summary and Analysis of Act Three

The third act takes place in the vestry room of the Salem meeting house, which is now serving as the anteroom of the General Court. Judge Hathorne asks Martha Corey if she denies being a witch, which she does. She claims to not know what a witch is, to which he replies "how do you know, then, that you are not a witch?"

From outside, Giles Corey shouts that Thomas Putnam is reaching out for land, but Danforth, the Deputy Governor, silences him. Giles forces his way into the court with Reverend Hale. Giles presents himself to Danforth and Hathorne, telling them that he owns six hundred acres and timber. Giles says he means no disrespect to the court, but he only meant that his wife was reading books, not that she was a witch.

Francis Nurse also presents himself, and tells Danforth that he has proof that the girls are frauds. Danforth reminds him that he has four hundred persons in jail upon his signature, and seventy-two condemned to hang. Mary Warren enters with Proctor, and Parris warns him that Proctor is mischief. Proctor tells Danforth that Mary Warren never saw any spirits, and he presents a deposition signed by Mary Warren that asserts this. Parris thinks that they have come to overthrow the court. Mary admits that her fits of bewitchment were pretense. Danforth questions Proctor, wondering whether he has any hidden intention to undermine the court. Cheever tells Danforth how Proctor ripped up the warrant, but Proctor says that it was only out of temper. Cheever also tells Danforth how Proctor plows on Sunday and does not come to church. Proctor asks Danforth if it strikes him odd that these women have lived so long with such an upright reputation only to be accused.

Danforth tells Proctor that his wife is pregnant; although Proctor did not know this, he tells them that Elizabeth never lies. Danforth agrees to let Elizabeth live another month so that she may show signs of pregnancy, and if she is pregnant she will live another year so that she may deliver.

Proctor submits a deposition to Danforth signed by ninety-one citizens attesting to their good opinion of Rebecca, Martha Corey and Elizabeth. Parris demands that these ninety-one be summoned for questioning, and claims it is an attack on the court. Hale asks if every defense is an attack on the court, but Parris tells him that all innocent and Christian people are satisfied with the courts in Salem. Mary Warren begins to sob. Hathorne reads the deposition, and asks which lawyer wrote it, but Giles says that he wrote it. He has been a plaintiff in thirty-three court cases, and thus has great experience with the law. Hathorne's father even tried a case of Corey's.

Mr. Putnam arrives, and Danforth tells him that there is an accusation that he prompted his daughter to cry witchery upon George Jacobs. Giles claims that the proof is that if Jacobs hangs for a witch he forfeits his property and only Putnam can buy it. Giles claims that someone told him that he heard Putnam say that his daughter gave him a fair gift of land when she accused Jacobs. Giles refuses to name this person, however. When Danforth threatens Giles with contempt, Giles responds that this is not an official court session. Danforth arrests Giles for contempt, and Giles makes a rush for Putnam, but Proctor holds him back. Proctor comforts Mary. Hale advises Danforth that he cannot say that Proctor is an honest man, but it would be better to send him home to hire a lawyer. Hale has signed seventy-two death warrants, and he claims that he dares not take a life without examining any reasonable doubt. He now doubts the guilt of Rebecca Nurse.

Danforth explains that witchcraft is by its very nature an invisible crime, thus only the witch and the victim will witness it. The witch will not accuse herself, thus one must rely on the victim. Parris wishes to question them, but Danforth tells him to be silent. Mary Warren claims that she is with God now, and Danforth tells her that she is either lying now or was lying earlier, and in either case committed perjury. Abigail enters with the other girls. Abigail tells Danforth that Goody Proctor always kept poppets. Proctor claims that he believes Abigail means to murder his wife, and orders Mary to tell Danforth how the girls danced in the woods naked. Parris tells Danforth that he never found anybody naked, but admits to finding them dancing. Parris demands that Mary Warren pretend to faint as she had done before, but she cannot, for she has no sense of it. She once thought she saw spirits, but now she does not.

Abigail threatens Danforth, claiming that the powers of Hell may affect him soon. Abigail pretends that she feels a sharp wind threatening her. Proctor calls Abigail a whore and grabs her by the hair. Finally he admits that he had an affair with Abigail. The court fears that if this is true, it finally provides a motivation for Abigail to be lying. Danforth orders Parris to bring Elizabeth to the court. If Elizabeth admits to firing Abigail for her affair with Proctor, Danforth will charge Abigail. Proctor is confident that his wife would never, could never lie, even to save him. But Elizabeth is questioned with her back towards Proctor so they cannot communicate, and she says that she fired Abigail because she displeased her, and because she thought that her husband fancied her. She says that Proctor never committed lechery. Proctor cries out for Elizabeth to tell the truth, that he has already confessed, but Danforth orders Elizabeth to leave.

Proctor says that his wife meant only to save his reputation. Hale claims that it is a natural lie to tell, and to stop before another person is condemned. Abigail then claims that she sees Mary Warren's spirit manifested as a bird, trying to hurt her. Mary Warren sobs that she is merely standing in court, but Abigail continues with the charade. Mary Warren claims that the girls are lying, but after Danforth threatens her and Abigail refuses to stop her charade, Mary submits and accuses Proctor of being the Devil's man. She says that Proctor made her sign the Devil's book and made her try to overthrow the court. Danforth orders Proctor to admit his allegiance with Satan, but Proctor cries out that God is dead, and that a fire is burning because the court is "pulling Heaven down and raising up a whore." Hale denounces the proceedings and quits the court.

Analysis

Amongst the characters in the play, it is Deputy Governor Danforth who seems to provide the most obvious symbol of Senator Joseph McCarthy. Danforth rules over the proceedings as if the accused are guilty until proven innocent, and adopts a harsh and vindictive air. However, Miller does not make Danforth a direct equivalent of the irrational demagogue McCarthy; rather, Danforth is a stern, cold man of unfailing faith in his judicial powers. He does not manifest any particular political ambition, but instead acts to preserve the strength of the court over which he rules. This does make Danforth suspicious of any attack on the plaintiffs and the proceedings, but also allows him some room for flexibility. He uses reason to persuade Proctor to drop his charges against Abigail, telling him that his wife is spared for at least a year and that he need not worry about her execution. It is Danforth's stern rationality that makes him a more disturbing figure; he is not a malicious villain equivalent to Abigail, but rather a man who has intense faith in the integrity of his court. He operates under the assumption that good and evil can be clearly and intensely defined, a flaw of tragic irony. In his desperate hope to sharply delineate good and evil, Danforth becomes the willing accomplice of those who obscure this line.

It is Reverend Parris who appears as the demagogue in this act of the play, denouncing all challenges to the court as challenges to Christianity and God himself. Parris is paranoid and foolish, demanding that all ninety-one people who attest to the good name of the three accused women be brought in for questioning. It is Parris' rabid defense of the trials that finally causes Hale to break from the court and offer a defense of the Proctors, Coreys and Nurses. Parris' demagoguery is placed into even sharper relief once the true reason for the girls' admission of witchcraft is revealed. Parris knows that the trials are a fraud and that the girls are lying, yet continues to push against witchcraft to suit his ends.

Miller develops the motivations of the proponents of the witchcraft trials in this chapter. Reverend Parris remains motivated by suspicion and paranoia, while Thomas Putnam moves from an original motivation of grudges against others to unabashed greed. Abigail Williams, in contrast, has moved from self-preservation to a more general lust for power. However, upon the arrest of Rebecca Nurse and Elizabeth Proctor, Reverend Hale now eschews the supernatural explanations for more concrete, legal explanations. He redeems himself from his role as a Pontius Pilate by serving as an advocate for justice. This is significant, for it provides concrete evidence that opposition to the trials does not necessarily mean opposition to law and order.

Deputy Governor Danforth espouses the central irony of the witchcraft trials: because there can be no concrete evidence of witchcraft, one must trust the word of the accuser as to whether any witchcraft has occurred at all. This essentially negates the idea of evidence, taking opinion and allegation to be concrete fact. It is this flaw on which Abigail Williams and the other girls capitalize when making their accusations.

Miller establishes that it takes only a simple accusation for a person to be convicted of witchcraft. Thomas Putnam uses this for economic gain, coercing his daughter into accusing George Jacobs so that he may purchase his land once Jacobs has been executed. Yet it is Abigail Williams who brings this particular quality into sharp relief. Abigail is intense and dramatic; she targets the weak-willed Mary Warren, knowing that she will easily break from her alliance with Proctor once challenged. When Abigail pretends to see a yellow bird attacking her, it is an obvious falsehood that is nevertheless admissible as evidence in this court of law.

The act ends by encompassing two central ironies. The first of these is that, to prove his own innocence and prove himself faithful to his wife, John Proctor must publicly declare his infidelity. To save Elizabeth and protect himself from an inevitable accusation of witchcraft, Proctor must tear down his name and condemn himself for the crime of lechery. Despite Proctor's obvious sin, this places Proctor as a martyr, sacrificing any chance for a good reputation in Salem, where public reputation is essential, in order to save his wife and others wrongly accused of witchcraft.

The second irony involves the testimony of Elizabeth Proctor. To save her husband's life, she must condemn him for lechery. Miller establishes that she is an honest woman who never lies, yet at the moment in which her honesty is most critical she chooses the noble yet practical lie, and defends her husband. As Hale notes, it is a natural lie for Elizabeth Proctor to tell, yet an incredibly ill-timed one; Elizabeth Proctor chooses dishonesty at the precise moment that her integrity matters the most.

Miller continues the theme of revolving accusations in this act when Mary finally breaks down and accuses Proctor of witchcraft. Fearful of her own life, Mary realizes that the only way to save herself is to accuse Proctor of coercing her into overthrowing the court. In this case the accusation contains some truth: Proctor did force Mary Warren into testifying - and yet, in this case the purpose is to promote true justice rather than to obscure it.

At the end of this act, Proctor condemns himself by claiming that God is dead. When he states this, he speaks metaphorically, lamenting a world in which the ostensibly just and moral society of Salem can be overthrown by one strong-willed girl. Once again Proctor gives in to melodramatics when faced with injustice. He may be correct, yet expresses his righteousness through means that make him an easy target for the likes of Abigail and Reverend Parris.

Summary and Analysis of Act Four

The fourth act takes place in a Salem jail cell later in the fall. Marshal Herrick enters with a lantern, nearly drunk, and wakes up Sarah Good. Tituba is also in the cell. She says that they will be going to Barbados as soon as the Devil arrives. Hopkins, a guard, tells them that the Deputy Governor has arrived. Danforth discusses with Hathorne whether it is wise to allow the increasingly mad-looking Parris to spend so much time with the prisoners. Cheever remarks on the many cows wandering the streets, now that their masters are in jail. Hale has been begging Rebecca Nurse to admit to witchcraft.

Parris arrives and tells Danforth that Abigail has vanished with Mercy Lewis. They have taken Parris' strongbox and he is now penniless. Parris claims that there are rumors of a rebellion against the witchcraft proceedings in Andover. Hathorne reminds Parris that all have been happy with the Salem executions, but Parris reminds him that Rebecca Nurse and John Proctor are respected members of the community and their executions will not be taken as well. Parris suggests postponing these hangings, and admits that there seems to be dissatisfaction, as shown by the low turnout at Proctor's excommunication.

Parris worries for his safety, having found a dagger at his doorway. Danforth refuses postponement, as it would show weakness on his part. Danforth summons Elizabeth Proctor. Hale tells Elizabeth that he does not want Proctor to die, as he would then consider himself a murderer. He tells Elizabeth that God damns a liar less than a person who throws one's life away. Elizabeth claims that this is a devil's argument, but Hale says that we are not capable of reading God's will. Danforth wonders if there is any wifely tenderness in Elizabeth. Elizabeth asks to speak with her husband. Herrick brings in Proctor, who is now bearded and filthy. Proctor asks about Elizabeth's unborn child and the boys, who are kept by Rebecca's son Samuel. Elizabeth tells Proctor that Giles is dead; he would not answer to his indictment and the court pressed him to death, laying stones on his chest until he pleaded aye or nay. His last words were "more weight."

Proctor asks Elizabeth what she would think if he confessed, but Elizabeth says that she cannot judge him. She says that she will have him do what he wishes, but she does want him alive. Proctor says that he cannot mount the gibbet as a saint, as he is not a saint like Goody Nurse. Elizabeth says that she has her own sins to account for, and blames herself for forcing her husband to turn to lechery. Proctor states to Hathorne that he will confess himself, but he asks Elizabeth once again if it is evil. She answers that she cannot judge, but he asks in return who will judge him. When they demand a written confession, Proctor asks why he must sign. Danforth says it is for the good instruction of the village.

The guards bring in Rebecca Nurse, who is astonished that John is confessing. Proctor refuses to say that he saw Rebecca Nurse in the Devil's company, or anybody else. Danforth demands that Proctor prove the purity of his soul by accusing others, but Hale advises that it is enough that he confess himself. Parris agrees, but Danforth once again demands that Proctor sign the document. Proctor says that he has confessed to God, and that is enough. He asks Danforth whether a good penitence must be public. Proctor asks how he can teach his children to walk like men when he has sold his friends. Proctor wishes to keep only his name, and Danforth thus refuses to accept his confession. Danforth orders Proctor to be hanged. Hale begs Elizabeth to plead with Proctor to sign a confession, but Elizabeth states that Proctor has his goodness now, and God forbid she take it from him.

Analysis

The fourth act of The Crucible largely concerns the perversion of justice that has occurred in Salem. Miller demonstrates this immediately in the comic interlude that opens the act. Tituba and Sarah Good are foolish comic foils whose claims of communing with Satan are intended to be absurd. Yet while these women are spared the gallows because they have confessed to witchcraft, those like Rebecca Nurse who refuse to admit to a crime they did not commit remain sentenced to execution. This large-scale inversion of justice is reflected in the larger workings of Salem society. As Parris claims, there is the possibility of rebellion because of the witchcraft trials, while the numerous people who remain in jail have caused the village to fall into shambles. This is yet another example of the irony of the witchcraft trials: while they meant to preserve the order of society, the trials throw Salem into a state of anarchy and rebellion.

However, since the previous act there has been a shift in the public opinion concerning the trials. Miller indicates that the citizens of Salem supported the trials when the victims were obviously disreputable members of the community, but the executions of respected figures like Goody Nurse are much more controversial. This reinforces the idea that the Salem witch trials were in part vindictive; the purpose of the trials was not to remove witches from Salem, but rather to remove certain members of the community for other reasons. For the citizens of Salem, the executions only become unacceptable when they involve those honored members of the community, even if the charges against them have the same proof, or lack thereof, as those against the disreputable Bridget Bishop or Sarah Osburn. The implications of this are wholly cynical: the shift in public opinion is not a turn toward justice but rather an expression of personal preference.

If there is a sense of justice in The Crucible, it is meted out to Reverend Parris and Abigail Williams in this act. Reverend Parris reveals himself to be a fool capable of being easily manipulated by Abigail Williams, whose guilt seems obvious thanks to her sudden escape from town and theft of Parris' savings. However, even with these revelations casting further doubt on the validity of Abigail's charges, the Salem court continues with the trials and executions. The trials have taken on a life of their own, separate from the accusations of the principals, who set legal machinations in motion that even they cannot stop. This fulfills the theme of snowballing accusations that

Miller established early in the play. The accusations began with Abigail Williams, but now, supported by the weight of the judiciary, the prosecution does not stop with her downfall.

Contrasting considerations of self-interest lead Danforth and Parris to beg John Proctor to confess to witchcraft. While Parris fears for his physical safety, Deputy Governor Danforth operates to defend the court from further attack. The change in Danforth's overt motivation is important. Previously, Danforth meant to uphold the integrity of the court, but here he suggests corruption to simply preserve the political stature of the government. Indeed, he even worries that postponing the executions would show the court's weakness. By prompting Proctor to give an obviously false confession, Danforth indicates that he likely believes that the witchcraft allegations are false. This fully demonstrates how the witch hunts have gained a life of their own; considerations of reputation and the political dynamic lead the court to continue with prosecutions and executions even when the original proponents of the trials are proven disreputable, and even when the political officials who run these trials show serious doubt in the validity of the charges.

The final passages of The Crucible concern ideas of martyrdom and justice. Miller places three of the accused as possible martyrs, each representing different methods and approaches to self-sacrifice. Giles Corey, the first of the noble victims of the trials, remains the comic tragedian even in the throes of his death. He does not passively accept the decision of the court, but struggles against the court's charges. Even when Giles Corey dies at the hands of the court, he chooses the mode of execution that will allow his sons to still inherit his property. In contrast, Rebecca Nurse accepts her fate passively, a long-suffering martyr to the court's injustice. Unlike the truculent Giles Corey, Rebecca Nurse only displays those most Christian qualities of resignation and turning the other cheek.

The critical test for John Proctor in this act is whether he will accept the martyrdom of Giles Corey and Rebecca Nurse or choose self-interest. Proctor himself proposes the question of whether a sinful man may accept martyrdom by clinging to principles he has not always upheld. The saintly Rebecca Nurse may accept martyrdom because it suits her character, but the sinful Proctor questions whether or not it is hypocrisy to stand for his principles when he is an overt sinner. Miller implies that Proctor may choose self-sacrifice because it is not a question simply of his reputation, but that of his family and his community. Proctor may not be an exemplar in all matters, but he could not serve as a father to his children if he were to so readily give up his name to preserve himself.

The second question of this act is whether it is a worse sin to lie to save oneself or to allow oneself to die. This is the fulfillment of the theme of self-preservation that has recurred throughout the novel. While Hale says that God damns a liar less than a person who throws his life away, Elizabeth calls this the devil's argument. Miller seems to support Elizabeth's position, for it is by giving self-preserving lies that Tituba and Sarah Good perpetuated the witch hunts.

Elizabeth Proctor serves as the moral conscience in this act of The Crucible. It is she who puts forth the most prominent arguments for Proctor accepting his own death, despite her stated wish that she wants her husband to remain alive. This could be interpreted as another manifestation of Elizabeth's cold nature, for she remains seemingly more concerned about abstract moral principles than her husband's life; Danforth even questions whether Elizabeth has any tenderness for her husband at all. Elizabeth is not to be played as a cold character, however. She refuses to influence her husband's decision despite her own wishes – he has earned her respect as a free moral agent, and she loves him all the more for his ability to make the right decision on his own.

The negotiations between Proctor and Danforth concerning his confession illustrate the theme of public versus private redemption. Proctor insists that his penitence remain private, while Danforth requires a public declaration of guilt and a further condemnation of other witches. It is this critical factor that allows Proctor to accept his martyrdom when he chooses to sacrifice himself to stop the perpetuation of the witchcraft accusations. Proctor thus answers his own concern about martyrdom, ending his life with an action that remains indisputably noble dispute the sins he has previously committed. He dies with his own name intact because, unlike so many others in front of the Salem court and the House Un-American Activities Committee, he refused to name names.

Suggested Essay Questions

1. **The Crucible is famous as a political allegory, but what exactly is Miller trying to say? Who do you think is being most criticized in the contemporary analogy?**

   Miller was particularly offended by those who "named names" before HUAC, and he himself refused to do so. While the Crucible indeed villainized the prosecutors and Court – those in the parallel positions of Joe McCarthy and HUAC – the play martyrs Corey and Proctor for refusing to do so. At the expense of their own lives, Corey and Proctor refused to condemn others, and in Miller's eyes this is the only truly moral decision.

2. **The Crucible features a significant reversal of social roles in the Salem community. Choose a character whose position of power is upended and analyze the development of their role in the town and in the narrative. Can you make any observations about gender in this process?**

   The witch trials greatly increased the power and agency of otherwise lowly women like Tituba and Abigail, while bringing down more respected community members like Rebecca Nurse and Elizabeth. The position of men remained more stable – they were always in charge, and even if some of them were executed for witchcraft they would always control the positions of highest authority.

3. **What is the role of gossip in the trials? How does Miller use gossip to implicate the whole town in the events of the witch trials?**

   Clearly the trials are begun by the wagging of tongues after the girls are found in the woods, but gossip certainly has a more enduring role. Reputations in Salem are made or broken based on slander and rumor, and reputation was a man's only defense against accusation – and even that often failed to correct aspersions. But gossip also proves to be a destructive force even in the hands of the good and unwitting, taking on a life of its own – Giles Corey, for instance, condemns his own wife simply by a slip of the tongue.

4. **Miller makes some significant changes to the historical events for the play – most noticeably, he raises Abigail's age from 11 to 19, and invents an affair between her and Proctor. What purpose does this serve?**

   The affair is a dramatic device. It provides motive for Abigail's accusation of Elizabeth, and complicates the relationship between the Proctors. By raising Abigail's age and giving her motives of revenge, Miller can complicate the characterization of what would otherwise be a tale-telling little girl, without compromising her villainy.

5. **Clearly, Proctor is the protagonist of the play, dominating three of the four acts. What begins as an ensemble rendering of the town's drama ends in an examination of a decision by one man, the focus gradually narrowed over the course of the play. How does Miller make this 17th century farmer into a character capable of holding our interest and sympathies for two hours?**

Proctor is developed as a "modern" figure in the play. He is resistant to authority, rebelling against both the church and the state. He sees through humbug and shouts it down. Moreover, he has a complicated relationship with his wife, and is flawed but in an understandable way. He is independent minded, and struggles against the conformity of Salem that is so like 1950s America. In short, he's like every other hero rebel – the same man in so many movies in stories, just realized this time in 17th century Salem.

6. **What started the Salem witch trials? In their contemporary parallel of the red scare, we know that there really were Communists. But in 17th century Salem, there was no true witchcraft. So how did this thing start, and what does Miller have to say about its origins?**

A major point of the play is that the witch trials were not truly started by any event or scandal – the discovery of the girls dancing in the woods was merely a tipping point, not the true origin. Miller is steadfast in his belief that the social structure of Salem is what caused the witch hunt and allowed it to accelerate. If it hadn't been Betty Paris falling sick after dancing in the woods, it would have been something else.

7. **Act One is punctuated by prose passages in which Miller details the background of Salem and the characters. However, this background mixes facts from the historical record with the changes Miller made for dramatic reasons. What do you think of this?**

Because the prose passages are contained within a fictionalized dramatic work, a reader should be aware that the passages are subject to the limitations of the form. However, Miller speaks with the voice of a historian in these passages, not with the voice of a playwright, and gives no indication that what he says is less than historical fact. Indeed, it is a slightly worrisome idea – a play about a man who died for the truth is so free with its own truths.

8. **What is the function of Reverend Hale in the narrative?**

Reverend Hale is an interesting and well-developed minor character. He serves the dramatic function of an outsider, aiding in exposition in the first act even as his presence catalyzes the witch trials. But in the third act, he begins to question the trials, and by the fourth act has renounced them completely and is actively working against them. Hale shows that the ministry and the courts need not all be evil, but that it is possible to realize the error of one's own ways and work to fix their effects.

9. **Mary Warren is a bit of a cipher – we see her only as a pawn of Abigail, and then of Proctor, and then again of Abigail. Do we learn anything about the "real" Mary Warren?**

Mary Warren is a particularly undeveloped character in the narrative, who functions largely as a plot device. We know that she is a weak-willed and terrified girl, who is easily manipulated by people stronger than herself. Abigail and Proctor are the ones who manipulate her, both threatening her with violence and vengeance, which draws a lucid connection between those two. Mary wants to be good, but she lacks the ability to see clearly where this good choice lies.

10. **Are the judges evil? Be sure to define what you mean by "evil" in your answer.**

This is a deceptively simple question. Miller believed that the judges in the witch trials were purely evil, and has stated that if he were to rewrite the play, he would make them less human and more obviously and thoroughly evil. But is evil a function of the will, or a failure of reason? These men did not set out to do evil – they legitimately saw themselves as doing God's work. Is it evil to be wrong? Arguably, the Putnams are the most evil characters in Miller's interpretation of the events, as they both support the trials and clearly are aware of the falsity of the charges.

Historical Dystopia   *Theme*

Many labels have been attached to The Crucible over the course of its life – tragedy, allegory, political screed, historical fiction, even horror. But the historical nature of the play often leads people to ignore its place in genre fiction, as a dystopia.

The dystopia is a sub-genre of speculative fiction, derived from its more philosophical cousin, the utopia. Sir Thomas More coined "utopia" in 1516 as a name for an ideal and impossible society. Pure utopias are rare in modern fiction, except as a Shangri-la or Brigadoon sought by characters from a non-utopian world. The significantly more popular genre of dystopia subverts the original concept by presenting worlds that either appear to be utopias but suffer from a fatal flaw (such as The Giver); worlds that are utopias to their inhabitants but unappealing to us (Brave New World); and worlds that are just plain awful (1984, and many others).

Generally, a dystopia shares significant tropes with science fiction, employing advanced technology and post-disaster scenarios to create the universe in question. But The Crucible is no less a dystopia for taking place in the past rather than the future, in a time of farmers and butter churns rather than zeppelins and thought control.

Arthur Miller was no stranger to borrowing and adapting tropes from other genres of theater and fiction. His first hit, All My Sons, took its cue from the naturalist style of Henrik Ibsen, and Death of A Salesman borrowed elements from Yiddish theater and magic realism. The Crucible plays as a straight historical, like Shakespeare's history plays, but the particular unfamiliarity of the historical setting and the allegorical political argument being constructed lead The Crucible to share many elements of the dystopian narrative.

Salem itself features many characteristics that are common of dystopian settings: strict social stratification, as in Brave New World; restricted sexuality and the melding of church and state, as in The Handmaid's Tale; minimal privacy and required conformity, as in 1984; and invasive political apparatus, as in Fareneheit 451. But by virtue of having actually existed, Salem itself cannot be a proper dystopia, by definition. Rather, The Crucible is a dystopian narrative, making use of the tropes of the genre to dramatize the real history of the Salem witch trials.

George Orwell's 1984 is widely considered the most influential and well-known dystopia, and as it was recently published and popular when Miller was writing The Crucible, it serves as a good example for comparing the structure of the play to the classic dystopia.

In the first section, or Act One, of 1984 we are introduced to the world of Big Brother, establishing the particular rules of this universe. Act One of the Crucible is much the same, showing us the context of Salem and its inhabitants and how things work in their society. Act Two of 1984 has the protagonist, Winston Smith, beginning to realize that the world he lives in is unequivocally bad, and tries to fight back against the system. Act Two of the Crucible likewise shows Proctor understanding how far the trials have gone, and planning to stop the courts. Act Three of 1984 brings Winston to O'Brien, and there is significant debate about the nature of his society. The Crucible's third act is the courtroom arguments about the validity of the trials and their evidence. Finally, 1984 finishes with the defeat of the hero and the bleak continuation of the dystopia. Although in some dystopias the hero succeeds in bringing down the system or escaping from his society, The Crucible is like 1984 in that its hero is also ultimately powerless in the face of the state, and is executed.

Aside from the structural similarity, The Crucible also shares characterization tropes with the dystopia genre. Like John Proctor, the hero of a dystopia is almost invariably a member of the society in question, usually fairly high in social standing, who instinctively understands that something is wrong with the world. He is generally a lone voice of reason, expressing the audience's opinion of the world in question. His rebellion often comes at great personal risk.

Moreover, a dystopia isn't merely entertainment. The point is to show the connection to the world the writer currently lives in, to exaggerate existing social and political flaws and demonstrate the damage they can do when taken to their logical extreme. Arthur Miller does just that – by framing 1692 Salem as a dystopia, he makes an even stronger case about the present day. Not only can political oppression and "naming names" lead to a dystopia-like environment – they have, in the true and not so distant past, in this very country. For that is the true point of the Crucible, to show just what depths society is capable of, now and in our past and in our future.

Author of ClassicNote and Sources

Jeremy Ross, author of ClassicNote. Completed on June 01, 2000, copyright held by GradeSaver.

Updated and revised Elizabeth Weinbloom June 15, 2008. Copyright held by GradeSaver.

Miller, Arthur. The Portable Arthur Miller. New York: Penguin Books, 1995.

Schlueter, June and James Flanagan. Arthur Miller. New York: Ungar Publishing Company, 1987.

Dukore, Bernard. Death of a Salesman and The Crucible: Text and Performance. NJ: Humanities Press International, 1989.

Siebold, Thomas (editor). Readings on The Crucible. San Diego: Greenhaven Press, 1999.

Martin, Robert A. "Arthur Miller's The Crucible: Background and Sources." Modern Drama, vol. 20, no. 3 (November 1977), pp. 279-90.

Bigsby, Christopher. "Introduction" (to the Crucible), Viking Penguin, 1995.

Budick, E. Miller. "History and Other Specters in The Crucible." Modern Drama, vol. 28, no.4 (December 1985)

Essay: Conformity, Imbalance of Power, and Social Injustice

by Geoff Cowper-Smith
June 05, 2001

A "Great Drama" is a play in which an audience can find personal relevance. It is something which an audience can relate to. A great drama should having meaning to audiences for multiple generations. Arthur Miller's "The Crucible" successfully related to its audience and left us with messages that still echo today. The Crucible must be considered to be a great drama because of Miller's skillful play writing which created a script that not only addressed the idea of conformity in American culture, but also illustrated the unreal amount of power that select individuals hold because they define the means by which we all live. These people make decisions on issues like what is considered to be right or wrong. These people have existed as long as history can acknowledge and during the period when The Crucible was first performed in America, this was a very current and delicate issue because of the actions of the House Un-American Activities Committee in Hollywood.

Conformity is an idea that has plagued mankind for ages. It is a strong theme in The Crucible, and Miller's audience can draw parallels to it in their own lives. In The Crucible, the need to conform to the church's views and that of its minister is quite evident. The characters in the play find themselves in a very difficult situation. They must either turn their backs on what they believe in and lie by admitting to having had "relations with the devil", thereby conforming with the church's wishes, or they must follow their individualistic beliefs and refuse to lie. This kind of pressure has been a theme throughout American culture forever. Miller was able to use this theme to make his audience think about where they would draw the line. People understood that these kinds of situations were around them everyday: was it more important to conform to company policy no matter what? Or was it more important to vocalize personal views, and risk getting fired? Was a person necessarily "bad" if they didn't live by the rules of the Church? Or was it alright to have ones own interpretations of those rules. These are just a few of the questions that people may have been asking themselves during the fifties. The Crucible should be considered a great drama just because of it's all encompassing theme of conformity. It is one which everyone will find personal relation to forever.

The Crucible has so much more to it that it needn't be considered great drama on the basis of a good theme alone. It also attacks the poor balance of power that we can see around us everyday. Miller shows us how much power a sole individual can have when that person defines the ideologies or beliefs by which we live. During the Salem Witch Trials religion was, much more so than now, the answer to what people didn't understand. So as a result, ministers and priests were extremely powerful because they were the only people that were "qualified" to interpret the rules of their religion. They were considered to be the voice of God. Back in Salem, how could anything have been more powerful than that? Nobody could question the priests because they would then be questioning God. Which of course was completely taboo. So a person in such a position of power could say nearly anything they wanted, such as deciding that "cleansing" was needed in Salem. And, as a result, people would listen and it would be done, but not necessarily deemed to be right.

In the 1950's the idea of an imbalance of power was still an issue. After just starting to recover from the Holocaust, which was fueled by the very same need for "cleansing" as in Salem but on a larger scale, Americans were bewildered as to how easily people could be manipulated by those in a position of great power. Hitler had just basically accused a few million people of being witches. Americans could see how weak they were. One could not question the government, the military, or the church. To this very day, a huge amount of people are still afraid of questioning the church - look at the issue of abortion and the Catholic Church's position upon it for example.

Miller portrayed the priests and judges in The Crucible as that certain type of people that Americans will always be up against in the struggle for power. While the Church and its' ministers isn't quite as powerful now because people can openly admit having no belief in God without fear of being hung, we now have a new group of people that decide what is true and what is not. Science is the new religion and scientists the new priests. Scientists are the only people capable of interpreting what all of the math and formulas mean. And as a result, the rest of us openly accept their conclusions to be the true. This is the same kind of reliance that people put on the church two hundred years ago. And at that time, you didn't question it. The church was always right. The Crucible is a great drama because it addresses the issue of conformity in American culture and questions the amount of power that we allow those to have whom are supposedly more educated than the majority of the population and are responsible for defining the ideologies and beliefs by which we live.

At the time when The Crucible was first being performed something was taking place that was very alike the Salem Witch Trials. In Hollywood, the House Un-American Activities Committee was investigating the film industry for communist activities. Actors, writers, and directors were interrogated as to whether or not they had involved themselves in any kind of relations with the Communist Party. If people didn't readily conform to the HUAC's line of questioning, and answer their questions regardless of whether or not they were deemed intrusive or not, it was assumed that they had been involved with the Communist Party. It was thought that the Communists were trying to gain control of the American film industry for propaganda purposes. As a result, those individuals that were thought to be in any way associated with the Communists were blacklisted in Hollywood and could no longer work there.

As history has shown us, the injustices that occurred during the Salem Witch Trials continue to go on. Most obviously by the HUAC in America at the time of Miller's

Essay: Conformity, Imbalance of Power, and Social Injustice

The Crucible. We see parallels between the Salem Witch Trials and other issues even today. Most recently, the military wanted to discharge any gay men in service. These kind of injustices will always exist. The Crucible addresses the idea of a group of select people choosing another group for a scapegoat to a supposedly determined "problem" that exists. This is yet another reason why The Crucible should be considered to be great drama.

Arthur Miller's, The Crucible, addressed issues which were as important to Americans in the 1950's as they are today. The idea of conformity is one which any given individual will always face. People who define the ideologies and beliefs by which we live will also always exist. As will the accusations made by one group of select individuals towards groups of others in order to support their cause, or solve their problem. The House Un-American Activities Committee was doing exactly that in the 1950's which was why the idea of "cleansing" in The Crucible was so relevant to Americans. Arthur Miller's play took on very strong themes and took a stand against issues that are still pertinent to date. Great drama is something in which an audience can find relevance and relation. Great drama is drama that will always be important. The Crucible is a play that no one will ever be able to ignore because of Miller's ability to touch issues and themes that have plagued mankind throughout history and will continue to do so in the future.

Essay: Conformity, Imbalance of Power, and Social Injustice

Essay: Sins and Ambitions

by Anthony Haddad
February 04, 2001

> "The belief in a supernatural source of evil is not necessary; men
> alone are quite capable of every wickedness." - Joseph Conrad

The Salem witchcraft trials illuminate a great human campaign to rid society of the wicked devil and his sinful messengers. However nobly intended, these trials create an era of fear and hysteria, generating an outlet for the evil persons of Salem to raise their reputations at the expense of the good. In effect, it becomes apparent that the accusers do not possess a power to prove another of a "Satanic alliance", but rather branch their motivations from ambition, a theory probed by Arthur Miller's play The Crucible. Afraid of the severe penalties for secretly dancing in the forest and chanting spells, characters such as Tituba and Abigail Williams accuse others of witchcraft for their self-preservation. Capitalizing on this newly acquired power, Abby's self-preservation transforms into a strong desire to do harm unto others and quench her great lust for power. Moreover, other individuals such as Thomas Putnam endanger the lives of others simply to satisfy their insatiable greed and self-interest. As a result, the accusers in the witchcraft trials become the embodiment of sin, fed by their varied ambitions.

Ironically enough, because Salem's stern religious ethic controls all aspects of society and promotes safeguards against all immoralities and sins, the townspeople are somewhat provoked to test these prevailing social values. This becomes the case with a group of young girls lead by Abigail Williams and Tituba, who secretly dance "like heathen in the forest" (1 10) and "conjure up dead spirits" (1 16), all tell-tale elements of witchery. Soon enough however, rumors spread and "the whole country's talkin' witchcraft", a definite "hangin' error" (1 19). Terrified, the girls entrap themselves in an atmosphere of hysteria and apprehension searching for the most painless means of ensuring their protection: shifting the blame onto someone else. Thus, in a climatic moment of confession led by Tituba, Abigail claims to "want to open [herself] " and embrace "the sweet love of Jesus" as well as announce the names of those who "trafficked with the Devil" (1 50). Consequentially, by lying, the girls become perpetual sinners; nevertheless, are able to reflect the severe punishments of witchcraft from themselves and uphold their self-preservation.

Coincidentally, the girls' initial identities as the vulnerable pawns of the devil's grand scheme rapidly transform into those of famed yet feared celebrities among the people of Salem. Taking this reality to her advantage, the opportunistic Abigail is able to expose her true malignant character by intentionally attempting to destroy the lives of others to satisfy her corrupt conscience. One such an example is her plot against Elizabeth Proctor, the wife of her former lover, John Proctor. "She is blackening my name in the village! She is telling likes about me! She is a cold, sniveling woman !"

(1 24). Expressing her grievances that stem from jealousy and extreme hatred, Abigail substantiates her need for revenge. Thus, Abigail testifies to the court that it was Elizabeth's "familiar spirit that stuck a needle two inches into the flesh of her [Abigail's] belly" (2 79). Because of the lack of any material evidence to disprove this claim, Elizabeth is automatically accused of witchcraft and taken away. Moreover, Abby's motivation for malevolence broadens even more to satisfy her growing hunger for control and authority and reassure herself of her above-the-law status. While in court, Abigail threatens, "Let you beware, Mr. Danforth. Think you to be so mighty that the power of Hell may not turn your wits? Beware of it!" (3 113) In this situation, Abigail declares herself as even a menace to a powerful and esteemed Judge, declaring her true prevailing authority even over a high-ranking official. Therefore, by developing and defining her true motivation for evil as doing harm to others as well as satisfying her interminable desire for power, Abigail is able to divulge the wide capacity of her truly wicked character.

Correspondingly, other people in the town of Salem also recognize the witch trials as an outlet to attain their varied desires and ambitions. Thomas Putnam, a wealthy farmer obsessed with his riches, uses and instigates the executions of others to profit economically. As a result, he is able to allow his incalculable greed and self-interest champion his morality and ethics. Putnam is said to have "coldly prompted [his] daughter to cry witchery upon George Jacobs" for "If Jacobs hangs for a witch he forfeit up his property And there is none but Putnam with the coin to buy so great a piece. This man is killing his neighbors for their land!" (3 101). Of course, although Putnam cautiously manages to deny the accusation, it is quite true that nothing more than his yearn for more land stimulates the execution of the innocent George Jacobs. Thus, as a slave to the pleasures of the materialistic world, Thomas Putnam is coldly able to condemn others of an undeserving execution because of his prevailing greed and self-interest, and in doing so, becomes the ultimate sinner.

The many accusers in the witchcraft trials succumb to the definition of sin itself, corruptly powered by their different ambitions. Thomas Putnam is hastily able to endanger the lives of others in order to satisfy his self-interest and his perpetual hunger for more, undermining any moral or ethical conduct he might uphold. The vile and opportunistic Abigail is able to unveil herself as a true dark, spiteful, and malicious individual that uses the witchcraft trials as an opportunity to ruin the lives of others as well as quench her undying lust for power. In a state of great fear and desperation, the naïve Tituba and Abigail are able to deflect the penalties of witchcraft off themselves and maintain their state of self-preservation. In conclusion, while the trials of life may deem some sinners champions, the trials of the eternal life have yet to come.

Quiz 1

1. **Why does Abigail Williams live with Reverend Parris?**
   A. She is his niece.
   B. She is having an affair with him.
   C. She is his servant.
   D. She is his illegitimate daughter.

2. **Which of these characters is not condemned for witchery?**
   A. Rebecca Nurse
   B. Bridget Bishop
   C. Giles Corey
   D. John Proctor

3. **Why does Reverend Parris wish to spare Proctor?**
   A. He is convinced that Proctor is innocent.
   B. He wishes to tear down the court.
   C. He wants to have revenge against Abigail.
   D. He fears for his life if a respected man is hanged.

4. **"The Devil is precise; the marks of his presence are definite as stone." What is the significance of this line?**
   A. It is ironic, for Reverend Hale is using ambiguous marks to define the devil's presence.
   B. It shows that Mary Warren is a prideful girl who thinks herself the superior of the Proctors.
   C. It foreshadows Giles Corey's death by stoning.
   D. It is a veiled threat that Reverend Parris uses against Proctor for opposing him.

5. **Which of the following did not occur during the dancing?**
   A. Susanna Walcott murdered a frog and a rabbit for Tituba's spell.
   B. Tituba attempted to conjure Ruth Putnam's sisters.
   C. Mercy Lewis danced naked.
   D. Abigail Williams drank a charm to kill Goody Proctor.

6. **"More weight." What of the following is not significant about this line?**
   A. Giles chooses his death, sacrificing himself to spare others.
   B. Elizabeth mentions this to John as he decides whether or not to admit to witchcraft, serving as an example of a friend who sacrificed himself for a greater good.
   C. Because Giles dies by refusing to answer questions, he is not excommunicated and dies a Christian.
   D. Danforth erroneously believes that Giles will admit to witchery if placed under greater torture.

7. **Which of the following characters does not support John Proctor's decision to falsely admit to witchcraft?**
   A. Reverend Hale
   B. Reverend Parris
   C. Elizabeth Proctor
   D. Deputy Governor Danforth

8. **Why do many of the accused admit to witchcraft?**
   A. They are forced to admitting to witchcraft under duress and torture.
   B. By admitting to witchcraft they guarantee that they will not be executed.
   C. They are actually witches.
   D. By admitting to witchcraft they can accuse others of the same crime.

9. **Which of the following is not a complaint that Proctor has against Reverend Parris?**
   A. Parris demands too much compensation, such as the right to his house.
   B. Parris reaches out for land at the expense of his neighbors
   C. Parris focuses on hell and damnation in his services.
   D. Parris wastes the church money on extravagant items.

10. **"Your justice would freeze beer." To whom does this line refer?**
    A. Thomas Putnam
    B. Reverend Parris
    C. Elizabeth Proctor
    D. Deputy Governor Danforth

11. **What grudge do the Putnams not have against the Nurses?**
    A. Rebecca Nurse has never lost a child nor grandchild, while Mrs. Putnam has lost all but one of her children.
    B. The Nurses own land that the Putnams covet.
    C. The Nurses opposed the Putnams' choice for minister.
    D. The Nurses and their allies broke away from Salem to form a new community.

12. **What does the commandment that Proctor forgets concern?**
    A. Murder
    B. Adultery
    C. Blasphemy
    D. Lying

13. **"What victory would the Devil have to win a soul already bad?" What is the significance of this line?**

    A. It foreshadows the eventual charges against respectable citizens such as Rebecca Nurse.

    B. It foreshadows Mr. Putnam's charges against George Jacobs.

    C. It shows that Reverend Parris suspects everybody of witchcraft.

    D. It is ironic, for the speaker is a lost soul charging others with villainy.

14. **What is the likely reason that Old Giles cannot say his prayers?**

    A. He is easily frightened.

    B. He is forgetful and barely knows his prayers.

    C. Rebecca Nurse sent her spirit out against him.

    D. His wife's reading blocks him from saying his prayers.

15. **"Theology, sir, is a fortress; no crack in a fortress may be accounted small." What is the significance of this line?**

    A. It shows that any person may be suspected of witchcraft for any small fault.

    B. It shows the hypocrisy of Reverend Parris, who himself has major flaws.

    C. It shows that Reverend Hale is invariably fixed on minor details.

    D. It shows the arrogance of the court in believing itself infallible.

16. **"The Crucible" is an allegorical tale that relates most strongly to which contemporary event for Arthur Miller?**

    A. The Holocaust

    B. The Nuremberg trials

    C. The McCarthy hearings

    D. The Starr report

17. **Which of the following is not evidence used by Hale against the Proctors?**

    A. Mary Warren's poppet

    B. John's affair with Abigail Williams

    C. The failure of their children to be baptised.

    D. The Proctor's absence from church.

18. **Which of the following is not matched to the person whom he/she accuses of witchcraft?**

    A. Abigail Williams : Elizabeth Proctor

    B. Tituba : Sarah Good

    C. Ann Putnam: Rebecca Nurse

    D. Betty Parris: George Jacobs

19. **Which character in the play is compared to Pontius Pilate?**
    A. Thomas Putnam
    B. Reverend Samuel Parris
    C. Reverend John Hale
    D. Giles Corey

20. **Which of the following is not matched to their motive for promoting the witchcraft trials?**
    A. John Hathorne : superstition
    B. Abigail Williams : lust
    C. Samuel Parris : paranoia
    D. Thomas Putnam : greed

21. **What is the significant about Danforth's support for Proctor's confession?**
    A. It shows that he knows that there are no witches in Salem.
    B. It shows that he will bend the rules whenever it suits him.
    C. It shows that his interest is in preserving the court and not in actual justice.
    D. It shows that he has turned against Putnam and Parris.

22. **Which character proclaims that Abigail Williams should be "ripped out of the world"?**
    A. Samuel Parris
    B. John Hale
    C. Elizabeth Proctor
    D. John Proctor

23. **Which line best represents Elizabeth Proctor's view in the trials?**
    A. "If Rebecca Nurse be tainted, then nothing's left to stop the whole green world from burning."
    B. "The shining sun is up, and them that fear not light will surely praise it."
    C. "Remember, until an hour before the Devil fell, God thought him beautiful in Heaven."
    D. "I cannot think the Devil may own a woman's soul when she keeps an upright way."

24. **What is significant about Giles Corey's charge against Thomas Putnam?**
    A. It is ironic, for Giles Corey is condemned for giving evidence that is hearsay, while equally invalid evidence is used to condemn persons for witchcraft.
    B. It illustrates the theme of the obscure division between public and private.
    C. It illustrates the theme of the novel of passing blame from one

character to another.

D. It is ironic, for Giles Corey charges Thomas Putnam with a crime for which Corey is guilty.

25. **What is the significance of the line "before the laws of God we are as swine! We cannot read his will."**

    A. This demonstrates the change in Reverend Hale, for at the beginning of the play he believed that he could ascertain any supernatural phenomenon.

    B. This demonstrates Proctor's contempt for the intellectual abilities of men.

    C. This is ironic, for Danforth believes that we can read God's will, or else he would not condemn people for witchcraft.

    D. When Elizabeth argues this, it shows that she does not want John to confess.

Quiz 1 Answer Key

1. (**A**) She is his niece.
2. (**C**) Giles Corey
3. (**D**) He fears for his life if a respected man is hanged.
4. (**A**) It is ironic, for Reverend Hale is using ambiguous marks to define the devil's presence.
5. (**A**) Susanna Walcott murdered a frog and a rabbit for Tituba's spell.
6. (**D**) Danforth erroneously believes that Giles will admit to witchery if placed under greater torture.
7. (**C**) Elizabeth Proctor
8. (**B**) By admitting to witchcraft they guarantee that they will not be executed.
9. (**B**) Parris reaches out for land at the expense of his neighbors
10. (**C**) Elizabeth Proctor
11. (**B**) The Nurses own land that the Putnams covet.
12. (**B**) Adultery
13. (**A**) It foreshadows the eventual charges against respectable citizens such as Rebecca Nurse.
14. (**B**) He is forgetful and barely knows his prayers.
15. (**A**) It shows that any person may be suspected of witchcraft for any small fault.
16. (**C**) The McCarthy hearings
17. (**B**) John's affair with Abigail Williams
18. (**D**) Betty Parris: George Jacobs
19. (**C**) Reverend John Hale
20. (**A**) John Hathorne : superstition
21. (**C**) It shows that his interest is in preserving the court and not in actual justice.
22. (**C**) Elizabeth Proctor
23. (**D**) "I cannot think the Devil may own a woman's soul when she keeps an upright way."
24. (**A**) It is ironic, for Giles Corey is condemned for giving evidence that is hearsay, while equally invalid evidence is used to condemn persons for witchcraft.
25. (**A**) This demonstrates the change in Reverend Hale, for at the beginning of the play he believed that he could ascertain any supernatural phenomenon.

Quiz 2

1. **"I think, sometimes, the man dreams cathedrals, not clapboard meeting houses." To which character does this refer?**
    A. Reverend Hale
    B. Thomas Putnam
    C. Reverend Parris
    D. John Proctor

2. **What is the explanation for Mary Warren's ability to faint in court?**
    A. She could faint because she was caught up in the excitement and commotion in court.
    B. She can faint at will, and used this to make herself seem more believable.
    C. She was afflicted by the witches, who sent out their spirits to harm her.
    D. She was afflicted with the same illness as Betty Parris that caused delusions and loss of consciousness.

3. **What is not significant about the poppet?**
    A. It demonstrates how a small, insignificant item can lead to a capital charge.
    B. It shows how weak-willed Mary Warren can be easily manipulated.
    C. It demonstrates that Elizabeth Proctor is a woman who clings to simple, childish pleasures.
    D. It shows that Abigail Williams is capable of premeditated murder.

4. **Which is not a reasonable explanation for the affair between Proctor and Abigail?**
    A. Elizabeth was sick for a long period of time.
    B. John Proctor was driven by an uncontrollable lust.
    C. Abigail Williams is an aggressive sexual predator.
    D. Elizabeth is a frigid, sexually distant woman.

5. **Which of the following does not describe of one of the first women accused of witchcraft?**
    A. Impoverished
    B. Alcoholic
    C. Pagan
    D. Promiscuous

6. **What is not significant about Danforth's demand that Proctor sign the statement?**
    A. It illustrates the theme of the division between public and private.
    B. It is ironic that Proctor wishes to keep his good name, for he already

sacrificed it when he confronted Abigail Williams.

C. The qualifications show that Danforth actually does not want Proctor to live.

D. It implies that Danforth knows that Proctor is not guilty of witchcraft.

7. **Which of these best represents the change in John Hale's views?**
   A. "Here is all the invisible world, caught, defined and calculated."
   B. "I dare not take a life without there be proof so immaculate no slightest qualm of conscience may doubt it."
   C. "While I speak Go'd law, I will no crack its voice with whimpering."
   D. "What victory would the Devil have to win a soul already bad? It is the best the Devil wants, and who is better than the minister?"

8. **Which of the following aspects of society did not contribute to the furor of the witchcraft trials?**
   A. An oppressive atmosphere toward sexuality.
   B. The lack of an opportunity for contrition and forgiveness.
   C. The disregard for legality and justice.
   D. The lack of a concrete distinction between public and private life.

9. **"I cannot pardon these when twelve are already hanged for the same crime. It is not just." What is significant about this line?**
   A. Danforth relies on an idea of justice, but in fact promotes injustice.
   B. It is ironic that the vindictive Parris would rely on ideas of justice.
   C. Danforth is beginning to show some weakness.
   D. It shows that Hale is in denial about the injustice he has committed.

10. **"Since 1692 a great but superficial change has wiped out God's beard and the Devil's horns, but the world is still gripped between two diametrically opposed absolutes." What is the significance of this comment by Miller?**
    A. This comment relates to the Cold War opposition between democracy and communism.
    B. This comment shows that concrete progress in society is not possible because of conservative forces.
    C. This comment shows that religious ideas are inherently part of human nature.
    D. This comment shows that society still adheres to Puritan principles but without the religious justification.

11. **Which character claims "I know not what a witch is"?**
    A. Rebecca Nurse
    B. Bridget Bishop
    C. Elizabeth Proctor
    D. Martha Corey

12. **Accusations against 'witchcraft' can be considered veiled attacks on all of the following values except?**
    A. Intellectual independence
    B. Individualism
    C. Sexual freedom

D. Communal living

13. **"There is a misty plot afoot so subtle we should be criminal to cling to old respects and ancient friendships." Which character states this line?**
    A. Reverend Hale
    B. Reverend Parris
    C. Abigail Williams
    D. Deputy Governor Danforth

14. **"There is blood on my head! Can you not see the blood on my head?" What is the significance of this line?**
    A. It shows that John Proctor has been tortured.
    B. It shows that Abigail can easily feign Satanic possession.
    C. It shows that Parris fears for his life.
    D. It shows that Reverend Hale feels guilty for h_s role in the trials.

15. **Which of the following lines shows that Elizabeth Proctor believes her husband should not confess to witchcraft?**
    A. "Whatever you will do, it is a good man does it."
    B. "Give them no tear! Tears pleasure them! Show honor now, show a stony heart and sink them with it."
    C. "It needs a cold wife to prompt lechery."
    D. "It come to naught that I should forgive you, if you'll not forgive yourself."

16. **What is Proctor's profession?**
    A. Farmer
    B. Lawyer
    C. Preacher
    D. Salesman

17. **Why has Corey been in court so much?**
    A. He often sues people
    B. He is often sued
    C. He likes it
    D. He is a lawyer

18. **What is Parris' profession?**
    A. Farmer
    B. Teacher
    C. Preacher
    D. Salesman

19. **What is Abigail's profession?**
    A. Servant
    B. Former servant
    C. Cook
    D. Prostitute

20. **What is Tituba's profession?**
    A. Cook
    B. Seamstress
    C. Slave
    D. Witch

21. **Why is Rebecca Nurse respected?**
    A. She has many children
    B. She is a preacher
    C. She has never assisted on a birth that didn't go well
    D. She has a lot of money

22. **What is Elizabeth's profession?**
    A. Farmer
    B. Wife
    C. Cook
    D. Seamstress

23. **What is Mary Warren's profession?**
    A. Servant
    B. Wife
    C. Seamstress
    D. Slave

24. **What is Mrs. Putnam's great loss?**
    A. Her children are mean
    B. She is unable to have children
    C. Only one of her children has survived
    D. All of her children are dead

25. **What is Francis Nurse's role in the trials?**
   A. Husband of an accuser
   B. Accuser
   C. Husband of a defendant
   D. Defendant

Quiz 2 Answer Key

1. **(C)** Reverend Parris
2. **(A)** She could faint because she was caught up in the excitement and commotion in court.
3. **(C)** It demonstrates that Elizabeth Proctor is a woman who clings to simple, childish pleasures.
4. **(B)** John Proctor was driven by an uncontrollable lust.
5. **(C)** Pagan
6. **(C)** The qualifications show that Danforth actually does not want Proctor to live.
7. **(B)** "I dare not take a life without there be proof so immaculate no slightest qualm of conscience may doubt it."
8. **(C)** The disregard for legality and justice.
9. **(A)** Danforth relies on an idea of justice, but in fact promotes injustice.
10. **(A)** This comment relates to the Cold War opposition between democracy and communism.
11. **(D)** Martha Corey
12. **(D)** Communal living
13. **(A)** Reverend Hale
14. **(D)** It shows that Reverend Hale feels guilty for his role in the trials.
15. **(D)** "It come to naught that I should forgive you, if you'll not forgive yourself."
16. **(A)** Farmer
17. **(A)** He often sues people
18. **(C)** Preacher
19. **(B)** Former servant
20. **(C)** Slave
21. **(A)** She has many children
22. **(B)** Wife
23. **(A)** Servant
24. **(C)** Only one of her children has survived
25. **(C)** Husband of a defendant

Quiz 3

1. **What is Goody Nurse's fate?**
   A. She confesses
   B. She is pressed
   C. She is acquitted
   D. She is hanged

2. **What is Giles Corey's fate?**
   A. He is acquitted
   B. He is hanged
   C. He confesses
   D. He is pressed

3. **What is John Proctor's fate?**
   A. He is acquitted
   B. He is hanged
   C. He confesses
   D. He is pressed

4. **What is Elizabeth's fate?**
   A. She confesses
   B. She is pressed
   C. She is acquitted
   D. She is hanged

5. **What is Tituba's fate?**
   A. She confesses
   B. She is pressed
   C. She is acquitted
   D. She is hanged

6. **What is Abigail's fate?**
   A. She is arrested
   B. She has a baby
   C. She is killed
   D. She runs away

7. Why are cows milling the streets?

    A. It's Free Cow Day

    B. Their owners are in jail

    C. Standards of property rights have declined

    D. The fences have been taken down to be used as gallows

8. Who is Hathorne?

    A. A lawyer

    B. The judge

    C. A preacher

    D. The sheriff

9. Who is Danforth?

    A. The deputy governor

    B. The judge

    C. The sheriff

    D. The minister

10. How is Reverend Hale different from Reverend Parris?

    A. He is a scholar

    B. He is from New York

    C. He went to Harvard

    D. He doesn't believe in witchcraft

11. Who does Corey accuse of land-grabbing?

    A. Parris

    B. Putnam

    C. Proctor

    D. Nurse

12. Who does Mercy Lewis work for?

    A. Parris

    B. The Nurses

    C. The Putnams

    D. The Proctors

13. Who does Mary Warren work for?

A. Parris

B. The Nurses

C. The Putnams

D. The Proctors

14. Why is Mrs. Corey arrested?

A. For flying

B. For reading books

C. For casting spells

D. For making potions

15. Why does Elizabeth lie to the court?

A. To save herself

B. To save John's life

C. To save John's reputation

D. To save time

16. What evidence does Giles Corey offer to the court?

A. Putnam is telling Mercy who to accuse

B. Parris is stealing cows

C. Goody Nurse gave his wife books

D. Abigail is threatening the girls

17. What is the petition that Proctor and Corey bring to the court?

A. Citizens attesting to Abigail's poor character

B. Citizens disagreeing with the conclusions of the court

C. Citizens requesting a new trial for Elizabeth

D. Citizens attesting to Elizabeth and Martha's good character

18. Why does Mary Warren tell the court about the girls' pretense?

A. Because she was tired of the pretense

B. Because she felt guilty

C. Because she was angry at Abigail

D. Because Proctor threatened her

19. Which thing didn't the girls do in the woods?

A. perform voodoo

B. try to contact the dead

C. dance naked

D. sing Barbados songs

20. What does Reverend Hale believe about witchcraft?

A. That there is no sure way to detect its presence

B. That it doesn't exist

C. That it has taken hold of Salem

D. That they must use scientific methods to identify it

21. Who made Elizabeth's poppet?

A. Tituba

B. Abigail

C. Elizabeth

D. Mary Warren

22. What did Abigail accuse Elizabeth of?

A. Pulling out her hair

B. Squeezing her lungs

C. Cutting slashes on her legs

D. Stabbing her in the stomach with a needle

23. Which commandment did Proctor forget?

A. Remember the sabbath

B. Adultery

C. Kill

D. Bear false witness

24. What are Giles Corey's last words?

A. No plea

B. I object

C. Just do it

D. More weight

25. **What does Elizabeth say John finally has at the end of the play?**
    A. His name
    B. His soul
    C. His purpose
    D. His goodness

Quiz 3 Answer Key

1. **(D)** She is hanged
2. **(D)** He is pressed
3. **(B)** He is hanged
4. **(C)** She is acquitted
5. **(A)** She confesses
6. **(D)** She runs away
7. **(B)** Their owners are in jail
8. **(B)** The judge
9. **(A)** The deputy governor
10. **(A)** He is a scholar
11. **(B)** Putnam
12. **(C)** The Putnams
13. **(D)** The Proctors
14. **(B)** For reading books
15. **(A)** To save herself
16. **(A)** Putnam is telling Mercy who to accuse
17. **(D)** Citizens attesting to Elizabeth and Martha's good character
18. **(D)** Because Proctor threatened her
19. **(A)** perform voodoo
20. **(D)** That they must use scientific methods to identify it
21. **(D)** Mary Warren
22. **(D)** Stabbing her in the stomach with a needle
23. **(B)** Adultery
24. **(D)** More weight
25. **(D)** His goodness

Quiz 4

1. **What animal does Abigail pretend to see?**
    A. A bat
    B. A cat
    C. A rat
    D. A bird

2. **Why is Elizabeth's execution postponed?**
    A. She has to testify against others
    B. She confessed
    C. She is pregnant
    D. Her guilt is questioned

3. **What does HUAC stand for?**
    A. House Un-American Action Commission
    B. House United Action Committee
    C. House Un-American Activities Committee
    D. House United American Commission

4. **The "witch hunts" of the 1950s were looking for whom?**
    A. Anarchists
    B. Communist sympathizers
    C. German spies
    D. Cult members

5. **Who led the anti-Communist hearings in the Senate?**
    A. Roy Cohn
    B. Edward R, Murrow
    C. Julius Rosenberg
    D. Joe McCarthy

6. **What did they call the list of Hollywood professionals who were barred from employment in the red scare?**
    A. The blacklist
    B. The Traitor list
    C. The Do-Not-Hire list
    D. The redlist

7. **Who first accused Martha Corey of reading strange books?**
    A. Putnam
    B. Abigail
    C. Cheever
    D. Giles Corey

8. **Who found the girls in the woods?**
    A. Parris
    B. Proctor
    C. Danforth
    D. Hale

9. **Who does not ask Proctor to save his own life?**
    A. Parris
    B. Danforth
    C. Elizabeth
    D. Hale

10. **Where is Hale from?**
    A. Boston
    B. Beverly
    C. Rockport
    D. Gloucester

11. **Where is Tituba from?**
    A. Tahiti
    B. Barbados
    C. The Dominican Republic
    D. Africa

12. **What year were the witch trials?**
    A. 1682
    B. 1689
    C. 1692
    D. 1699

13. In whose house does the play start?
   A. Parris
   B. Putnam
   C. Proctor
   D. Hale

14. What are Parris's sermons usually about?
   A. Hell and money
   B. Heaven and money
   C. Hell and politics
   D. Heaven and politics

15. When did The Crucible open on Broadway?
   A. 1953
   B. 1959
   C. 1963
   D. 1969

16. What religion were the people in Salem?
   A. Presbyterian
   B. Puritan
   C. Amish
   D. Wiccan

17. What makes Betty wake up and scream?
   A. Abigail asking her to wake up
   B. Hearing the Lord's name
   C. Seeing a cat
   D. Abigail beating her

18. How long before the start of the play did Abigail leave the Proctors?
   A. One week
   B. One month
   C. Two years
   D. Seven months

19. **What would "freeze beer"?**
    A. A witch's power
    B. Abigail's heart
    C. A Massachusetts winter
    D. Elizabeth's justice

20. **Why can't Mary faint for the court?**
    A. She is being bewitched
    B. Proctor is holding her
    C. Abigail scares her
    D. She doesn't have the feeling for it

21. **What does Abigail say is a "deadly sin"?**
    A. Lechery
    B. Bigotry
    C. Jealousy
    D. Lying

22. **Who accuses Proctor of witchcraft?**
    A. Tituba
    B. Abigail
    C. Mercy Lewis
    D. Mary Warren

23. **Proctor says they're pulling down heaven and raising up what?**
    A. A whore
    B. Hell
    C. A baby
    D. Death

24. **Why is Parris worried for his safety in the fourth act?**
    A. He was attacked
    B. He realized he was in the wrong
    C. He received death threats
    D. He found a dagger at his door

25. What does Proctor not have to do to confess?

A. Accuse others
B. Demonstrate his ability to do witchcraft
C. Make public penitence
D. Sign a statement

Quiz 4 Answer Key

1. **(D)** A bird
2. **(C)** She is pregnant
3. **(C)** House Un-American Activities Committee
4. **(B)** Communist sympathizers
5. **(D)** Joe McCarthy
6. **(A)** The blacklist
7. **(D)** Giles Corey
8. **(A)** Parris
9. **(C)** Elizabeth
10. **(B)** Beverly
11. **(B)** Barbados
12. **(C)** 1692
13. **(A)** Parris
14. **(A)** Hell and money
15. **(A)** 1953
16. **(B)** Puritan
17. **(B)** Hearing the Lord's name
18. **(D)** Seven months
19. **(D)** Elizabeth's justice
20. **(D)** She doesn't have the feeling for it
21. **(C)** Jealousy
22. **(D)** Mary Warren
23. **(A)** A whore
24. **(D)** He found a dagger at his door
25. **(B)** Demonstrate his ability to do witchcraft

ClassicNotes

GradeSaver™

Getting you the grade since 1999™

Other ClassicNotes from GradeSaver™

1984
Absalom, Absalom
Adam Bede
The Adventures of Augie
 March
The Adventures of
 Huckleberry Finn
The Adventures of Tom
 Sawyer
The Aeneid
Agamemnon
The Age of Innocence
The Alchemist
Alice in Wonderland
All My Sons
All Quiet on the Western
 Front
All the King's Men
All the Pretty Horses
The Ambassadors
American Beauty
Angela's Ashes
Animal Farm
Anna Karenina
Antigone
Antony and Cleopatra
Aristotle's Ethics
Aristotle's Poetics
Aristotle's Politics
As I Lay Dying
As You Like It
Astrophil and Stella
The Awakening
Babbitt
The Bacchae
Bartleby the Scrivener

The Bean Trees
The Bell Jar
Beloved
Benito Cereno
Beowulf
Bhagavad-Gita
Billy Budd
Black Boy
Bleak House
Bless Me, Ultima
The Bloody Chamber
Bluest Eye
The Bonfire of the
 Vanities
The Book of the Duchess
 and Other Poems
Brave New World
Breakfast at Tiffany's
The Brothers Karamazov
By Night in Chile
Call of the Wild
Candide
The Canterbury Tales
Cat's Cradle
Catch-22
The Catcher in the Rye
The Caucasian Chalk
 Circle
The Cherry Orchard
The Chocolate War
The Chosen
A Christmas Carol
Chronicle of a Death
 Foretold
Civil Disobedience

Civilization and Its
 Discontents
A Clockwork Orange
The Color of Water
The Color Purple
Comedy of Errors
Communist Manifesto
A Confederacy of
 Dunces
Confessions
Connecticut Yankee in
 King Arthur's Court
The Consolation of
 Philosophy
Coriolanus
The Count of Monte
 Cristo
Crime and Punishment
The Crucible
Cry, the Beloved
 Country
The Crying of Lot 49
Cymbeline
Daisy Miller
Death in Venice
Death of a Salesman
The Death of Ivan Ilych
Democracy in America
Devil in a Blue Dress
Dharma Bums
The Diary of a Young
 Girl by Anne Frank
Disgrace
Divine Comedy-I:
 Inferno
A Doll's House

For our full list of over 250 Study Guides, Quizzes,
Sample College Application Essays, Literature Essays and E-texts, visit:

www.gradesaver.com

ClassicNotes

Getting you the grade since 1999™

Other ClassicNotes from GradeSaver™

Don Quixote Book I
Don Quixote Book II
Dr. Faustus
Dr. Jekyll and Mr. Hyde
Dracula
Dubliners
East of Eden
The Electric Kool-Aid
    Acid Test
Emma
Ender's Game
Endgame
The English Patient
Ethan Frome
The Eumenides
Everything is Illuminated
Fahrenheit 451
The Fall of the House of
    Usher
Farewell to Arms
The Federalist Papers
For Whom the Bell Tolls
The Fountainhead
Frankenstein
Franny and Zooey
Glass Menagerie
The God of Small Things
The Good Earth
The Grapes of Wrath
Great Expectations
The Great Gatsby
The Guest
Gulliver's Travels
Hamlet
The Handmaid's Tale
Hard Times

Heart of Darkness
Hedda Gabler
Henry IV (Pirandello)
Henry IV Part 1
Henry IV Part 2
Henry V
Herzog
The Hobbit
Homo Faber
House of Mirth
House of the Seven
    Gables
The House of the Spirits
House on Mango Street
Howards End
A Hunger Artist
I Know Why the Caged
    Bird Sings
An Ideal Husband
Iliad
The Importance of Being
    Earnest
In Our Time
Inherit the Wind
Invisible Man
The Island of Dr. Moreau
Jane Eyre
Jazz
The Jew of Malta
The Joy Luck Club
Julius Caesar
Jungle of Cities
Kama Sutra
Kidnapped
King Lear
The Kite Runner

Last of the Mohicans
Leviathan
Libation Bearers
Life is Beautiful
Light In August
The Lion, the Witch and
    the Wardrobe
Lolita
Long Day's Journey Into
    Night
Lord Jim
Lord of the Flies
The Lord of the Rings:
    The Fellowship of the
    Ring
The Lord of the Rings:
    The Return of the
    King
The Lord of the Rings:
    The Two Towers
A Lost Lady
Love in the Time of
    Cholera
The Love Song of J.
    Alfred Prufrock
Lucy
Macbeth
Madame Bovary
Manhattan Transfer
Mansfield Park
MAUS
The Mayor of
    Casterbridge
Measure for Measure
Medea
Merchant of Venice

For our full list of over 250 Study Guides, Quizzes,
Sample College Application Essays, Literature Essays and E-texts, visit:

www.gradesaver.com

ClassicNotes

Getting you the grade since 1999™

Other ClassicNotes from GradeSaver™

Metamorphoses
The Metamorphosis
Middlemarch
Midsummer Night's
  Dream
Moby Dick
Moll Flanders
Mother Courage and Her
  Children
Mrs. Dalloway
Much Ado About
  Nothing
My Antonia
Mythology
Native Son
Night
No Exit
Notes from Underground
O Pioneers
The Odyssey
Oedipus Rex or Oedipus
  the King
Of Mice and Men
The Old Man and the Sea
On Liberty
On the Road
One Day in the Life of
  Ivan Denisovich
One Flew Over the
  Cuckoo's Nest
One Hundred Years of
  Solitude
Oroonoko
Othello
Our Town
Pale Fire

Paradise Lost
A Passage to India
The Pearl
Phaedrus
The Picture of Dorian
  Gray
Poems of W.B. Yeats:
  The Rose
Poems of W.B. Yeats:
  The Tower
The Poisonwood Bible
Portrait of the Artist as a
  Young Man
Pride and Prejudice
The Prince
Prometheus Bound
Pudd'nhead Wilson
Pygmalion
Rabbit, Run
A Raisin in the Sun
The Real Life of
  Sebastian Knight
Red Badge of Courage
The Remains of the Day
The Republic
Rhinoceros
Richard II
Richard III
The Rime of the Ancient
  Mariner
Robinson Crusoe
Roll of Thunder, Hear
  My Cry
Romeo and Juliet
A Room of One's Own
A Room With a View

Rosencrantz and
  Guildenstern Are
  Dead
Salome
The Scarlet Letter
The Scarlet Pimpernel
Secret Sharer
Sense and Sensibility
A Separate Peace
Shakespeare's Sonnets
Shantaram
Siddhartha
Silas Marner
Sir Gawain and the
  Green Knight
Sister Carrie
Six Characters in Search
  of an Author
Slaughterhouse Five
Snow Falling on Cedars
The Social Contract
Something Wicked This
  Way Comes
Song of Roland
Song of Solomon
Sons and Lovers
The Sorrows of Young
  Werther
The Sound and the Fury
The Spanish Tragedy
Spring Awakening
The Stranger
A Streetcar Named
  Desire
The Sun Also Rises
Tale of Two Cities

For our full list of over 250 Study Guides, Quizzes,
Sample College Application Essays, Literature Essays and E-texts, visit:

www.gradesaver.com

Made in the USA
Monee, IL
09 October 2020